Are Predatory Commitments Credible?

A volume in the series Studies in Law and Economics

edited by William M. Landes and J. Mark Ramseyer

Previously published:

Politics and Property Rights: The Closing of the Open Range in the Postbellum South
by Shawn E. Kantor

More Guns, Less Crime: Understanding Crime and Gun-Control Laws
by John R. Lott, Jr.

Japanese Law: An Economic Approach
by J. Mark Ramseyer and Minoru Nakazato

ARE PREDATORY COMMITMENTS CREDIBLE?

Who Should the Courts Believe?

John R. Lott, Jr.

The University of Chicago Press • Chicago and London

JOHN R. LOTT, JR., is the John M. Olin Law and Economics Fellow at the
University of Chicago. He has held positions at Stanford, UCLA, Wharton, Rice,
and Texas A&M and was the chief economist at the United States Sentencing
Commission during 1988 and 1989. He is the author of *More Guns, Less Crime:
Understanding Crime and Gun-Control Laws* and of over seventy articles in
academic journals.

The University of Chicago Press, Chicago 60637
The University of Chicago Press, Ltd., London
© 1999 by The University of Chicago
All rights reserved. Published 1999
08 07 06 05 04 03 02 01 00 99   1 2 3 4 5

ISBN 0-226-49355-5 (cloth)

Library of Congress Cataloging-in-Publication Data

Lott, John R.
    Are predatory commitments credible? : who should the courts believe? / John
R. Lott, Jr.
    p. cm.
    Includes bibliographical references and index.
    ISBN 0-226-49355-5 (cloth : alk. paper)
    1. Predatory pricing—United States. 2. Antitrust law—United States. I.
Title.
    HF5417.L67   1999
    338.5'22—dc21   98-32261
                                                                              CIP
⊚ The paper used in this publication meets the minimum requirements of the
American National Standard for Information Sciences—Permanence of Paper for
Printed Library Materials, ANSI Z39.48-1992.

To Gertrud

CONTENTS

Can we empirically distinguish predation from competitive behavior? How likely is predation by private firms? Are government enterprises more or less likely to predate than private firms? This book answers these wide-ranging questions.

A vast literature already exists on predation, and the predominant direction during the last decade has been to increasingly employ game-theoretic models. Such models have been used to demonstrate the possibility of extensive predation. Yet, a major drawback with models based upon game-theory is that they are typically very sensitive to their assumptions. In other words, more or less any result is possible when the assumptions are altered even slightly. Almost any outcome in terms of price and quantity movements can be interpreted as predatory or competitive behavior, depending on the model chosen. Game theory may have contributed a certain "richness" to the analysis of industrial organization, but it has done so at the cost of tractability. Good theories may well be complicated, but ultimately they must generate clear testable implications to be of much practical use.

This book critically analyzes the existing types of predation theories as well as the empirical work on the subject. I show how the results crucially depend on some key assumptions, in particular asymmetrical information between the incumbent and the potential entrant. I argue that many of the game-theoretic models are more applicable to government enterprises than to private firms.

The second major task of this book is to provide new empirical evidence that allows us to differentiate among different theories of firm behavior. In contrast to the previous literature on predation by private firms, I test the key assumptions (rather than the implications) behind game-theoretic models of predation. Further, I offer statistical evidence to test whether game theory can explain which firms get charged with predatory pricing.

I received helpful comments from seminars at Brigham Young   *ix*

University, Emory University, the Federal Trade Commission, George Mason University School of Law, Northwestern University Law School, Southern Methodist University, UCLA, University of Chicago, University of Georgia, University of Pennsylvania (Economics and Wharton), University of Toronto, the 1994 American Law and Economics Association meetings, the 1992 Southern Economic Association meetings, the U.S. Department of Justice, and the 1991 Western Economics Association meetings.

I wish to thank Robert Hansen (whose work went into the material presented in chapter 5) and Tim Opler (whose work helped provide the basis for chapter 2). Discussions with Andrew Dick were also very important to my work on chapter 4. The influence of Armen Alchian, Dennis Carlton, Harold Demsetz, Ben Klein, Sam Peltzman, and George Stigler can also be seen throughout the book. Many of the ideas in this book are based upon by previously published research: "Testing Whether Predatory Commitments Are Credible," *Journal of Business* 69 (July 1996): 339–382; "Profiting from Induced Changes in Competitors' Market Values: The Case of Entry and Entry Deterrence," *Journal of Industrial Economics* 43 (September 1995): 261–271; "Predation by Public Enterprises," *Journal of Public Economics* 43 (November 1990): 237–251; and "Are Government Enterprises More Likely to Engage in Dumping?: Some International Evidence from Dumping Cases," *Managerial and Decision Economics* 16 (May–June 1995): 15–204. I would also particularly like to thank my wife, Gertrud Fremling, whose counsel and advice enhanced the entire book. The John M. Olin Law and Economics Program at the University of Chicago School of Law also provided valuable financial support for this project.

ONE

The Debate on Predation

In 1980, the predominant view among economists was that predatory price cutting would rarely if ever be profitable (see Bork 1978, East-erbrook 1981, and McGee 1958 and 1980). Their view can be simply stated: predation is costly. A predatory firm must not only cut its price below cost for the units already being produced, but must also expand its output at this low price. The increased quantity is neces-sary to drive down the price competitors can charge. According to these economists, even if predators succeed in driving away competi-tors, the fruits of this costly victory would prove short-lived. The only way for predatory firms to profit is to drive away competitors so that they can charge high prices. Yet, raising prices lures new firms to enter, which forces the incumbent predator again to drive these new entrants from the market. The losses incurred from predatory pricing are shown to exceed any subsequent profits from monopoly prices. Numerous other problems can face the predator. For example, even if a competitor is successfully eliminated through bankruptcy, the specialized assets remain intact and can be put to use by another competitor.

The U.S. Supreme Court's 1986 Matsushita decision has made pros-ecution of predation cases very difficult (Liebeler 1986). However, in the last decade, many game-theoretic papers have argued that preda-tion can be a profitable strategy.[1] With asymmetric information and other appropriate assumptions, game theorists have shown that—at least theoretically—it can pay for an incumbent firm to manipulate potential entrant beliefs about the returns to entry, even when cost and demand conditions remain unchanged (see Milgrom and Roberts 1982b, Kreps and Wilson 1982, Rasmusen 1991, and Roberts 1986). Acquiring a so-called reputation for toughness can be used to discourage later entry. Initial losses from predatory price cuts serve as a reputational investment in convincing outsiders that entry is costly, and the payoff comes later when the firm earns monopoly rents. More recent models of predation build on reputational stories where last periods problems are not so important (e.g., Tirole 1990, 112 and 122–126).

Predation is theoretically possible, but whether predation is in practice profitable is an entirely different question.[2] Despite a large and growing theoretical literature, few empirical studies have been undertaken. While some economists like Klevorick (1993, 166) castigate the courts for not relying more on game theory, other game theorists such as Ordover and Saloner (1989) seemingly concede that the alternative game-theory scenarios are so numerous that straightforward applications by the courts are essentially impossible. Yet, the implications and key assumptions underlying the models must be examined and validated before they can serve as a guide for policy purposes.

As is well recognized, though seldom discussed, the implications of game-theory models are extremely sensitive to their assumptions. Furthermore, many of the most widely adopted assumptions are questionable in and of themselves. For example, the game-theoretic literature typically assumes incumbents to be the ones with the asymmetric informational advantages. While incumbents probably do have certain first-mover advantages, challengers obviously enjoy the advantage of knowing whether and when they might enter the market. Jack Hirshleifer, in his 1971 *American Economic Review* article, demonstrates this sensitivity in the area of inventions: inventors can at least partially internalize the social returns to their discoveries by investing in assets where the asset's price would likely rise after the invention became known. Hirshleifer's simple idea has important implications for predation. Firms can profit by trading in the securities of other companies whose values are influenced by their firm's actions (such trading is legal in the United States). Take the case of entry: if a predatory firm suffers greater losses than the entrant when entry takes place, it might pay for potential newcomers to short sell the stock of the predatory firm and enter the market. Since potential entrants presumably must know better whether they will enter a market, this reverses the normal game-theoretic assumption: now it is potential entrants who possess the informational advantage over predators.[3]

However, even if predatory behavior is generally found to be unprofitable or irrational, it does not necessarily imply that rules against predation ought to be abolished. Richard Posner (1976, 187) argued that even if predation is "irrational," "it would not follow that predatory pricing should be freely permitted. The correct level of an activity is achieved by compelling the actors to bear the full social costs of their actions, including their mistakes, and the predator's losses may not equal those costs." Posner's argument requires only that these so-called irrational firms typically respond to incentives. Yet, any evaluation must examine not only whether "irrational" crimes are prevented, but also whether courts incorrectly penalize and discourage efficient nonpredatory activities. Are laws against predation primarily used to penalize efficient firms or those engaging in predation?

The game-theoretic models can also be used for comparing private firms with government enterprises. Predation by private firms hinges on their credibly committing themselves to predation and communicating that commitment to all potential entrants. Some have argued that such predatory reputations are based on an asymmetric information advantage: the predatory firm knows its own objective function better than anyone else does (Milgrom and Roberts 1982b, 285). Potential entrants can therefore sometimes be fooled into believing that the established firm is not a profit maximizer, but rather values other dimensions, such as market share. The potential entrant would then take the threats of reduced prices seriously and decline entry. The established competitor would then be left alone to maximize not just its ordinary profits but its *monopoly* profits. However, given that the reason that established firms are predatory is really to increase profits, it is unlikely that all potential entrants assume that such firms operate according to some behavioral rule other than strict profit maximization. If all potential future entrants are not sufficiently convinced that entry will initiate further predation, predation will prove costly without generating much (if any) benefit.

In contrast to private firms, government agencies are more typically viewed as not being profit maximizers but trying to meet other objectives, such as maximizing the bureau's size or output. Several reasons why a public enterprise would maximize its output rather than its profits have been advanced. Since profit-based incentive-compensation schemes for managers are not allowed and monitoring is costly, managers of public enterprises may try to maximize output or discretionary budgets because these strategies often yield benefits to public employees. A larger output can raise salaries, open greater future opportunities to consult or contract with the agency after retirement, increase utility (if the bureaucrat intrinsically values the mission of the agency), as well as increase prestige from being associated with a larger agency. Yet, despite the empirical evidence that suggests that such behavior persists, the shirking explanations are unsatisfactory. Output maximization should presumably be just as visible to the politicians who monitor agency behavior as it is to economists who study these questions, and if this behavior truly constituted an agency problem, there would undoubtedly be pressure from voters and politicians to counteract a tendency to it. It is necessary to explain why politicians do not sufficiently counteract an agency problem. As I explain later, it is plausible that predatory behavior by public enterprises can maximize political support.

I. Existing Evidence of Predation by Private Firms

Despite a great many game-theoretic models, there are few empirical studies of predation, and these studies provide no systematic evidence confirming the assumptions of the models or substantiating the predictions. The main drawback is the failure to differentiate predatory results from what would be observed in perfectly competitive markets.

Few economists attempt to predict firm behavior—perhaps because of the obvious multiplicity of equilibriums resulting from these models. In his trenchant review of the *Handbook of Industrial Organization,* Peltzman (1991, 207) writes:

> I was struck by the variety of questions that arise in formulating and solving game-theoretic models—questions whose answers can crucially affect results. Here is a nonexhaustive list gleaned just from this chapter: (1) How many players are there? (2) Who moves first? (3) Who remembers what (e.g., are there information lags)? (4) Who knows what (e.g., is knowledge common or private)? (5) When do they know it? (See also question 3 above.) (6) Who can communicate with whom and when? (7) What is the probability of any outcome? (8) How reasonable are the players? (9) Is choice once and for all or subject

to change over time? If subject to change, in how many periods? (10) How long is each period? (11) What is the discount rate? (12) How long do players live? (13) How do players today respond to past play (e.g., do players develop reputations)? (14) Does an equilibrium exist? (15) Is equilibrium coalition proof? (See question 1 above.) (16) Is equilibrium robust to changes in assumptions? (17) How are deviations punished? (18) Is there a continuum of reactions or a discrete number? (19) Are the players' reaction functions smooth or discontinuous? (20) What does player A believe about B's objective function and vice versa?

As Peltzman recognizes, not all of the questions must be answered all the time, but many of them must usually be dealt with and the results from a model are frequently crucially affected. Although in theory these are interesting questions, what price do economists pay for this "richness"? Do the models help us predict behavior? Or are we left with many possible models that can "explain" virtually any given set of results? If we can find an explanation in game theory for *any* set of results, how could the theory ever be proved wrong? If a theory can never be falsified, can we ever show it to be correct?

When so many different game-theoretic models produce the same predictions and we cannot test the models easily, it is possible to show that what typically appears as the most innocent and desirable competition can indeed be consistent with undesirable strategic behavior. As Carlton and Perloff (1990, 422) write:

> passing along cost savings through lower prices, investing in research and development in order to lower costs, the gathering of marketing information, and arranging distribution channels for a product are all desirable features of competition that are difficult to distinguish from some of the strategic behavior that has been described. Moreover, even when strategic behavior can be isolated, it is conceptually very difficult to distinguish undesirable from desirable strategic behavior.[4]

It was once considered a virtue of economics that a simple powerful notion—for example, demand curves slope downward—could explain so many phenomena (see e.g., Alchian and Allen 1983, 13–44). Now we have many tools and many ways of analyzing a problem, but the range of behavior that economists feel comfortable explaining appears to be smaller. Increasingly "case studies" are being used to show that a particular model is consistent with a real-life case that occurred in an industry. This is an unfortunate development because anything can be proved. Expressed in statistical terms, the obvious problem is that many regression lines can be fitted through a single point.[5]

Burns's (1986) paper tries to be an exception to this trend. He attempts to provide systematic empirical evidence on the reputations that firms garner from past predatory actions. Between 1891 and 1906, the American Tobacco Company and two affiliated firms acquired 43 of their competitors. Burns states that, to acquire the assets of victims of predation as well as the competitors not yet preyed upon, predatory pricing by the Tobacco Trust during those years lowered the price by about 25 percent. His evidence has frequently been taken as proof that predators can acquire a reputation to follow through on predatory commitments (see e.g., Tirole 1990 and Baker 1994).

As Burns himself notes, however, his results are also consistent with perfectly competitive behavior. If the lower prices were instead due to lower cost production resulting from the mergers, the value of less efficient rival firms should also decline. Mergers might either reflect successful predatory acts or create lower costs of production. In later work Burns (1989) reaffirms the difficulty in distinguishing predatory behavior from perfect competition in his earlier results, and he turns to anecdotal evidence from executive testimony to argue that successful predation attempts were indeed occurring in the Tobacco Trust case.

Weiman and Levin (1994) also provide evidence of predatory behavior, the case of the Southern Bell Telephone Company from 1894 to 1912. However, again, like Burns, the authors acknowledge (p. 114) that the empirical evidence is equally consistent with a competitive explanation. Their empirical work consists of regressions on telephone prices immediately before and after new entry. They found that prices fell immediately prior to a competitor's entry and fell still further once entry took place (p. 111). Their preferred interpretation is that the initial drop in prices prior to entry was a predatory attempt to discourage the new firm from entering. This is quite plausible. Southern Bell's profits may have declined immediately prior to new entrants coming into the market and then declined still further once actual entry occurred precisely because they were engaged in predatory pricing. Yet, a competitive explanation is equally plausible. According to a competitive market interpretation, the promise of future entry may have convinced many potential telephone subscribers to delay obtaining service until competitors had entered and prices therefore had been driven down. Southern Bell simply could no longer charge monopoly prices as the market became increasingly competitive.

Again like Burns, Weiman and Levin ultimately relied upon anecdotal evidence to argue that the observed pricing patterns were predatory. However, the anecdotal evidence in both studies is open to alternative interpretations.[6] The practical usefulness of their evidence is further becoming increasingly limited as some courts have begun to argue that "intent is not a basis for liability ... in a predatory pricing case" (*A.A. Poultry Farms, Inc. v. Rose Acre Farms, Inc.,* 881 F.2d 1396 (7th Cir. 1989)). What might appear to some observers as evidence of successful predation can be viewed by others as mere intentions of vigorous above-marginal cost competition. Managers cannot be expected to express themselves in internal memos in the precise manner that economists or judges prefer.[7]

Other work has unsuccessfully tried to provide systematic evidence of effective collusion. While collusion itself is not a central topic of this book, the inability to differentiate competitive explanations from collusion is worth illustrating. In one particularly well-known and frequently cited example, Robert Porter (1983) tests whether the changes in railroad prices for shipping grain from 1880 to 1886 can be explained by temporary breakdowns in the Joint Executive Committee Railroad cartel. He finds that output increased and prices fell when these price wars occurred. Since he uses price wars (as defined by the *Railroad Review*) as a proxy for periods when the cartel broke down, he also finds—not surprisingly—that it was related to cartels supposedly breaking down. This is a serious mistake. It represents a big logical jump to claim that periods of lower prices and higher outputs are by definition periods when a cartel breaks down. While his evidence is indeed consistent with his hypothesis, it is clear that generally lower prices and higher outputs have nothing at all to do with a cartel temporarily breaking down. For instance, nobody would claim that retail clearance sales should be defined as periods when cartels have broken down. Prices plummeting during clearance sales might well reflect a rather inelastic demand curve for an individual firm. Does this imply a cartel with a lot of monopoly power?

Further, Porter does not account for the opportunity costs of shipping grain, as his regressions fail to include measures for the supply

of alternative cargo that the railroads could be carrying. Any significance placed upon prices falling when new railroads enter the market
is also problematic. As Michael Darby and I (1989) have noted, new
entrants may lower their prices below what appears to be the marginal cost simply to encourage customers to try the product and to
create a reputation for high quality products or service.

While anecdotal or case study stories of predation are fairly common (e.g., Yamey 1972), the case for predation primarily rests on
only a couple of well-known case studies. From an economic perspective, the most fascinating and surely longest debated example of
predatory pricing involves John D. Rockefeller's Standard Oil Company. Between 1870 and 1879, Standard Oil's market share of U.S.
refined petroleum grew from 4 to 90 percent. McGee's 1958 and 1980
papers probably present the best-known refutation of the frequent
claim that Standard Oil behaved like a predator, acquiring companies
under threats of predation. McGee particularly points to the entry of
new competitors (e.g., Lewis Emery) after the initial mergers took
place.

In a recent article, Granitz and Klein (1996) present the most per-
suasive anecdotal evidence to argue that Standard Oil was acting as
a predator. According to them, McGee's evidence of new entry after
mergers is misleading. Citing testimony in the Standard Oil case, they
write that "the evidence indicates that Emery was squeezed out of
refining twice" and that his entry into the refinery business was not
typical (p. 38, fn. 100). They also point out that if Standard Oil
achieved its dominant position through "voluntary" merger and acquisition, individual refiners would have been better off remaining
outside the cartel and free-riding on the higher monopoly prices produced by Standard Oil (p. 2).

Instead Granitz and Klein provide a completely different story:
The Erie, the Central, and the Pennsylvania railroads essentially allowed Standard Oil to enforce a cartel agreement among themselves.
Whenever a railroad cheated on the cartel, it was up to Standard Oil
to pressure the wayward carrier through the threatened loss of crude
oil shipments. In return for enforcing the cartel, Standard was given
preferential shipping rates, thus leaving its competitors little option
but to agree to being acquired by Standard. This explanation fits the
theory of raising rivals' costs advanced by Salop and Scheffman
(1987). All Standard Oil had to do was offer a competitor a payment
that exceeded the next best use of the competitor's facilities.

Yet, it is difficult to accept uncritically this explanation for Standard Oil's success in taking over so much of the oil industry. For example, why didn't the railroads charge Standard Oil for the privilege of enforcing the cartel agreement? The scenario implies that the railroads gave Standard Oil the large profits associated with the privileged shipping rates without any compensation in return. Even as late as 1874, 60 percent of the U.S. refining market was controlled by Standard Oil's competitors, and it would appear that the railroads still should have been able to replace Standard Oil with another firm willing to enforce the cartel for a smaller share of the profits.

More puzzling is why the railroads continued to let Standard Oil proceed with its mergers and acquire progressively larger market shares. What could the railroads have gained by allowing Standard Oil to obtain a monopoly on oil production? What they would lose is fairly obvious. They risked creating a successive monopoly problem, and as the non-Standard Oil share of oil production shrank, the monopoly shipping rates the railroads were able to charge on this progressively smaller share would produce less income.[8] Perhaps the railroads simply made a mistake by too readily giving Standard Oil such a valuable role without making the company pay for this privilege. Or perhaps they simply failed to understand that letting Standard Oil acquire all of its competitors would cut the railroads' own long-term profitability.

Even if Granitz and Klein are correct, other puzzles remain. Was petroleum the only product that could be used to ensure maintenance of the cartel? If cartelization through a third-party firm was so effective, why have not other railroads or other industries employed this technique? Finally, in other places where collusive railroad practices were attempted, substantial entry by new railroad competitors took place (Kolko 1965). If collusive railroad practices were really the explanation for the Standard Oil case, why don't we observe a similar pattern of new entry here?

The Tobacco Trust and Standard Oil cases have received a great deal of attention from economists because they appear to be the most obvious examples of predation. However, it must be remembered that these often cited cases represent only a small portion of the predation charges brought since the Sherman Act passed in 1890.

Using the CHH Trade Regulation Reporter, Roland Koller (1971) found that 123 federal antitrust cases were decided between 1890 and 1965. In twenty-eight of these cases the defendant was acquitted on other than procedural grounds. Out of the other ninety-five cases, twenty-three produced both a conviction and a factual record that was sufficient to judge whether predation had occurred. Using the ambiguous standard of whether the accused firm had reduced its price below its short-run average total cost, Koller claimed to find evidence that predatory price cutting was attempted in only seven cases, that it succeeded to some extent in four, and that it had a harmful effect upon resource allocation in only three, where predation led to either merger or collusion. Using "such data as was available" for the other seventy-two cases, Koller (p. 111, fn. 8) believes that similar findings would be produced there also.

Even if we ignore concerns raised by Bork (1978, 155) over whether these three cases truly represented predation, the returns to using courts to ferret out predation appear to be small. Unfortunately, Koller's evidence indicates that firms were held liable in sixteen cases when there was no attempt to predate. Furthermore, the three cases that were said to harm consumers involved either mergers with overwhelming shares of the market or collusion—activities that were already prohibited by other antitrust laws.

II. Recent Supreme Court Decisions and the Possible Future

> If the court errs by condemning a beneficial practice, the benefits may be lost for good. Any other firm that uses the condemned practice faces sanction in the name of stare decisis, no matter the benefit. If the court errs by permitting a deleterious practice, though, the welfare loss decreases over time. Monopoly is self-destructive. Monopoly prices eventually attract entry. (Easterbrook 1984, 1–2)

With the notable exception of *Eastman Kodak v. Image Tech. Services*,[9] the Supreme Court has been very skeptical of game-theoretic models of monopoly power.[10] Yet, despite the Matsushita decision, predatory charges against firms are continuing. During the 1990s, well-known cases have included Brown & Williamson in the cigarette industry as well as American Airlines—both were accused of unfairly lowering prices to drive out competitors.[11] More recent concerns have been raised against Microsoft and a proposed U.S. Department of Transportation actions against the four largest airlines (American, Northwest, Delta, and United).[12]

The Brown & Williamson case is probably the most interesting since it is the only one where a jury not only found the company guilty of predatory behavior but also imposed a large penalty ($148.8 million). This case was also heard by the Supreme Court, and it allows us to understand where the Court currently stands on these issues.[13] At the request of Topco, a wholesale buying organization for retail grocers, the Liggett Corporation began producing "generic" or private label cigarettes for Topco in 1980. This move was such a success that Liggett began offering its own line of generic cigarettes to other customers, and by early 1984 Liggett's generic brand accounted for 4 percent of the total cigarette market. Responding to this success, R. J. Reynolds and Brown & Williamson introduced their own discount and generic brands. The ensuing price war between Liggett's and Brown & Williamson's generic cigarettes precipitated the predation suit brought by Liggett. Liggett offered estimates of Brown & Williamson's revenue and cost figures, indicating that, during the first eighteen months Brown & Williamson charged prices below average variable costs.

Liggett's legal complaint was that Brown & Williamson's below-cost pricing was strategically aimed either to force its smaller rival out of the generic cigarette market and thus allow Brown & Williamson to raise prices later, or to have Liggett passively acquiesce to higher prices. The aim was allegedly to stem the flow of consumers to discount cigarettes from the more lucrative full-revenue brands.

There were many assumptions behind Liggett's claims. For example, Brown & Williamson with only 12 percent of the U.S. market could hardly be classified as a "monopolist," and while it would bear the full costs of driving Liggett from the market, it would obtain only a small share of the benefits from the higher prices that might be obtained on full-revenue brands.[14] Liggett claimed that all the cigarette manufacturers (presumably including itself) were in tacit collusion with regard to full-revenue brands and that once the threat of generic brands was removed, supracompetitive prices would again be charged. Yet, no explanation was offered for why Brown & Williamson would have been willing to bear the entire costs of predation while sharing the benefits with the rest of the industry. Indeed, by 1992, Philip Morris had 42 percent of the market followed by R. J. Reynolds with 29 percent, both standing to benefit much more from any future price increases than comparatively tiny Brown & Williamson with only 12 percent.[15]

The Supreme Court's Brown & Williamson decision continued the reasoning first set forth in Matsushita, where the Supreme Court for the first time focused not only on whether firms might be operating below cost, but also on whether it was possible for the supposed predator to recoup these losses.[16] To prove price predation, a plaintiff must demonstrate that the predator had a "reasonable prospect" (the Robinson-Patman Act standard for primary-line price discrimination) or "dangerous probability" (the Sherman Act Section 2 standard for attempted monopolization) of recouping the costs of predation.[17]

The question is whether the losses are larger than the potential monopoly profits. To answer this, the Court has focused on a set of economic variables such as: the length of the predation period, how far the predator's prices are below cost, the predator's ability to absorb the output of target firms, and entry conditions in the relevant market. Like Matsushita, Brown & Williamson involved cartels, which the court pointed out made recoupment less likely. The "Areeda-Turner test" of whether predators are pricing below average variable cost is still important today, but it is now relegated to the first stage of deciding whether predation has occurred. A plaintiff must also show that the alleged predator is able to recoup its losses by exercising monopoly power.

Brown & Williamson was the first ever decision where the Supreme Court set aside a jury verdict in an antitrust case. This sent a powerful signal on the Court's views of what constitutes predation. Because of the strong evidence provided by Liggett, some analysts have drawn the far-reaching conclusion that the Court's opinion "may have brought something else to a close: all predatory pricing cases" (Glazer, 1994, p. 45).[18]

The Brown & Williamson case also illustrates just how radically the Supreme Court's opinions on predation have changed over the years. In the 1967 Utah Pie case, the Supreme Court held that predatory intent could be inferred from nothing more than bellicose language in defendants' internal memos or from declining prices caused by the defendants' pricing practices. No attention was paid to whether an accused predator could actually succeed in monopolizing the market. Indeed this led many to object that the Court's decision "obstruct[ed] vigorous price competition."[19]

Yet, with all the recent activity by the Justice Department against Microsoft, it is probably too early to predict the end of predation cases.[20] Microsoft not only is giving away its internet browser but is paying people to use it.[21] Microsoft's claim that it will never charge a price for the browser was meant to allay fears of possible future monopoly pricing in the event competitors such as Netscape were driven from the market. Yet critics are not satisfied with this response since bundling the browser with Windows would allow Microsoft to charge more for the operating system.[22]

In the Microsoft case, the issue of predation is further complicated by claims that this market is affected by "network externalities and path dependence." Network externalities means that one person's decision to purchase a product is influenced by the number of other users. Just as with fax machines—where more people with faxes increases the returns to others having fax machines—, internet browsers are more valuable when there are more compatible web pages. Since the benefits increase with the number of users, an aspect of natural monopoly enters into the analysis: large networks are perceived to have advantages over smaller ones. Network externalities and natural monopolies are hardly new from a theoretical standpoint, and would therefore not complicate any discussion of predation. Indeed, by definition, a natural monopoly would ultimately lead to the same outcome as perfectly executed predation. However, this would not be detrimental, because under the conditions of a natural monopoly having only one firm is the "natural" (i.e., efficient) solution (albeit possibly with some regulation).[23]

In the Microsoft case analysts are concerned that once consumers adopt a particular technology or software, they will be "locked in" even when superior technologies exist (Lopatka and Page, 1995, and Liebowitz and Margolis, 1995b). While everyone might desire to switch, it is difficult for any one individual to switch because of the lack of other users. Each individual supposedly waits for others to move first, with the result that no one purchases the new and better software.[24] Yet, if it is natural for a lock-in to occur, why would a "lock-in" from Microsoft's browser be worse than one from Netscape? Some argue that the browser provides a substitute environment to conventional operating systems, and thus generates more of a "lock-in" when there is neither a competing operating system nor a browser.[25]

The general concern is that society inadvertently gets stuck with undesirable technologies. Indeed, Paul David (1992, 137) argues that "The accretion of technological innovations inherited from the past therefore cannot legitimately be presumed to constitute socially optimal solutions provided for us—either by heroic enterprises or herds of rational managers operating in efficient markets." Several lawyers along with economists Garth Saloner and Brian Arthur (Reback et al. 1995) state the predatory threat we face from Microsoft in apocalyptic terms: "It is difficult to imagine that in an open society such as this one with multiple information sources, a single company could seize sufficient control of information transmission so as to constitute a threat to the underpinnings of a free society. But such a scenario is a realistic (and perhaps probable) outcome." For these authors, technological choice should be a concern of antitrust policy, not something left to the randomness of the market.

"Lock-ins" supposedly have occurred for other products. Yet closer examination repeatedly reveals problems with these claims. One of the most prominent examples is the QWERTY layout of the typewriter keyboard. According to Paul David (1985), who popularized this example, a supposedly "accidental set of happenings" resulted in a clearly inferior keyboard layout being adopted. However, Liebowitz and Margolis (1990) provide a fascinating and detailed story about the intense competition between proponents of various keyboard layouts before QWERTY won out as the standard. More important, the alternative unadopted keyboard by Dvorak turned out not to be the paragon of efficiency that David had claimed. The Navy study that David relied upon was severely flawed and not unbiased— Dvorak was the Navy's own top expert in the area that the report fell under, and he had a large financial stake in the study's findings.[26]

New evidence does not support the claim that typing speeds are higher on the Dvorak keyboard, let alone fast enough to compensate for the costs of switching layouts (Liebowitz and Margolis 1990, 15–18). Analogous claims have been made in the past, and have been refuted, about the superiority of BETA over VHS (Liebowitz and Margolis 1995a), and of narrow- over broad-gauge railroads (Hilton, 1990), as well as about the initial adoption of AM radio (Vita and Wellford 1994).[27] In fact, the success of the VHS despite its being introduced after BETA provides evidence against the "lock-in" hypothesis.[28]

The theoretical discussion of "lock-ins" is also weak. Customers or competing firms are typically regarded as being locked into undesirable products simply because of their own lack of foresight.[29] If such lack of foresight was important, it is difficult to explain how

CD players, automobiles, or most other new technologies ever got started. After all, the first CD players had almost no disks, the first automobiles did not have ready access to gas stations, and CD-ROMs initially had little software. Clearly both consumers and producers formed some expectations of the future that rendered these products successful. Presumably the providers of technologies are hardly helpless. They can also influence the outcome between competing technologies by doing such things as giving away free samples in order to demonstrate their value. The strongest technologies have the most to gain from these comparisons.

Nor is it obvious that consumers value a larger number of other users without regard to who those users might be. For example, some large corporations might be sufficiently large that they can internalize the advantages of superior technology. Indeed as Liebowitz and Margolis (1995b) point out, the first fax machines were used primarily by companies wishing to send information or pictures within the firm itself. It might even be advantageous for the company to be the only one to use faxes.

While the discussion about "path dependence" is currently very topical, without concrete examples its popularity is likely to be short-lived. In the past, economists have frequently exhibited a great deal of faith in their ability to reorganize markets. Years ago economists would have pointed to electricity generation, cable television, or telephone service as classic examples of natural monopolies. There was always a certain irony that firms in these industries were granted exclusive monopolies and protected from competition when the theory would predict that no one would want to enter in against such "natural monopolists" (Hazlett, 1985). Yet, with deregulation and increased competition, even these examples can no longer be viewed as natural monopolies. Therefore, the arguments favoring price regulation in these markets have become equally doubtful.

The tying arguments are equally unconvincing.[30] Microsoft does have monopoly power in the market for operating systems, but forcing customers simultaneously to purchase both the operating system and the browser will not hurt the customers. There are two possibilities to consider. If the web browser is merely bundled in with the operating system, the impact is basically nonexistent since Netscape is now offering its own browser free.[31] If integrating the operating system and browser would somehow prevent customers from using alternative browsers, forcing them to use only its own web browser (if indeed some customers regard the browser as inferior) would lower the price that Microsoft could charge for its operating system.

Microsoft's dominance of other markets like word-processing and spreadsheet software has not resulted in any easily observable harm to customers in terms of higher prices, lower quality, or stalled innovations. Indeed these markets have seen in large permanent reductions in prices (Liebowitz and Margolis, 1999). Since Microsoft obtained the dominant share of sales in word processing in 1992 the average price of word processing software has fallen by almost 70 percent, reversing an upward trend. Spreadsheet prices have declined by about 60 percent after Microsoft's Excel displaced Lotus in 1993 as the leading spreadsheet producer. These large price declines may be the real explanation for the hostility of Microsoft's competitors.

During the last couple of decades, the courts have been quite skeptical of recognizing what might simply be ordinary competition between firms as predation. What competitors have claimed as predation, courts frequently have viewed as just the normal give-and-take of competition. This book shows that the courts generally have held the correct view on these issues. Whether courts continue to resist the dire predictions of their failure to reshape our technology markets remains to be seen. However, what is clear is that once the courts accept the claims of "lock-ins" and the belief that antitrust policy is well suited to choose tomorrow's technology, there are few obvious dividing lines to limit future intervention.[32]

III. Outline of the Book

The next chapter discusses some of the theoretical assumptions behind these game-theoretic models when applied to private firms. I examine whether the assumptions necessary for the Milgrom and Roberts (1982b), Kreps and Wilson (1982), and Tirole (1990, 122–126) models have any basis in reality. For example, simply hiring managers who value market share or output maximization is insufficient if managers can be removed when it actually becomes necessary to engage in predation. Firms must also make it difficult to remove the managers or alter their compensation schemes. I test the assumptions behind the models which argue that managerial preferences prevent last period problems that arise during predation and those more recent reputational models where there are no last periods. I find no evidence that allegedly predatory firms are organized as these game-theoretic models imply. If anything, the reverse seems to be frequently true.

The third and fourth chapters apply some assumptions of the reputational models regarding opponents' perceptions of a predatory firm's objective functions to where they would seem to belong most logically. If these assumptions about a manager's objective function are believable, I attempt to show that they are most believable in an area economists have ignored: government enterprises. The fourth chapter tests whether government enterprises are more likely to engage in predatory behavior than private firms. This is done by examining international dumping complaints and comparing how often such complaints are brought against different types of firms from different countries.

In chapter 5, I ask how sensitive the standard results are to the assumptions that if asymmetrical informational advantages exist, they exist on the side of the incumbent. As this chapter has emphasized, game-theoretic models involve a multitude of assumptions both explicit and implicit. Why predatory firms are assumed always to have informational advantages is not obvious. For example, can potential entrants make money using information on their decision to enter a market with a predatory firm and can these entrants use the predatory firm's commitment to lose money to increase the returns to entry? In fact, this chapter shows that the more credible the commitment that a predator will follow through on his threat, the greater is the return to entry. Several historical examples are used to illustrate the perils that predatory firms face.

TWO

Reputational Models of Predation: Testing the Assumptions

A prominent method that firms employ for altering others' beliefs about them involves acquiring a "reputation for toughness" through predation to discourage later entry (Milgrom and Roberts 1982b and Kreps and Wilson 1982).[1] Initial losses from predatory price cuts serve as a reputational investment in convincing outsiders that entry would prove costly. The payoff from this investment comes later when firms earn rents in the absence of entry. While these models show that predation is theoretically possible, whether predation is in practice profitable depends on many explicit and implicit assumptions about the real world. It is important that the plausibility of key assumptions underlying these models be examined and validated before the models are used for policy purposes.

Making predation strategies credible (in recent terminology "re-negotiation-proof") requires that firms ensure that managers who proceed with costly predatory acts are not penalized financially or ousted from office for doing so. Thus, if firms neither provide financial incentives to increase output when entrants attempt to enter nor guarantee executive job security, predators cannot credibly deter entry. Otherwise, entrants will recognize that it will be unprofitable for the incumbent to fulfill predatory threats. In this chapter I investigate how plausible the reputational theories of predation are. To do this I carry out two tests asking the same question: did firms taken to court on predation charges have the ability to make a predatory commitment? My tests examine managerial compensation and entrenchment in firms that have been accused or convicted of predation.

The remainder of this chapter proceeds as follows. Section II discusses what is required to make predatory threats credible. I discuss how management salary structures and job security should vary across firms in an industry with a predatory firm. Predictable implications are drawn not only for the traditional Milgrom and Roberts and Kreps and Wilson type story, but also for more recent vintages of these models involving signaling false information, a variant of the long purse hypothesis suggested by Telser (1966), and reputational models related to Klein and Leffler's (1981) quality premium hypothesis. Section III uses this theoretical discussion to study empirically whether firms convicted or merely accused of predation possess the characteristics necessary for predation.

II. Creating a Reputation for Toughness

A. Credible Commitments, Compensation, and Entrenchment

What incentive do managers have to create a reputation for retaliating against potential entrants? While shareholders may enjoy the rewards of future rents when establishing a reputation for predation, the manager may suffer if his compensation is tied to the firm's short-run profitability.[2] A solution is simply to align the manager's interests with those of the stockholders by properly structuring the manager's compensation contract. The most obvious method is to vary the manager's compensation so that it reflects the effect of the manager's actions on the firm's stock value. This would give the manager the correct incentives, provided that the market had at least as good information as potential competitors about his firm's commitment to future retaliation.

Alternatively, firms might hire managers who value other things besides maximizing profits. For example, managers who highly value the company's market share should be more likely to reduce prices when new entry occurs.[3] This approach follows some theoretical models where predatory behavior depends on the competitors' believing that the predatory firm has a particular type of manager. However, since incentive-based pay—rather than flat salaries—is nearly universal among managers, firms obviously do not rely exclusively on managers' nonmonetary preferences to ensure outcomes.

It is crucial that predatory firms provide managers with incentives to expand output at the expense of accounting profits during predatory periods. If entry occurs, the ability to increase output greatly and maintain it at a higher level is central to any predatory strategy.

Potential entrants must be made to believe that there is some probability that incumbent managers value maximizing market share. Managers who increase output in the face of entry should thus be rewarded for doing so. Relating salaries to short-term swings in profits is more costly to predatory firms than to nonpredatory firms, since the former incur large short-run losses while driving entrants from the market. Evidence that firms accused of predatory behavior pay their managers less when either output increases or short-term profits fall would cast doubt on whether those managers could credibly commit to predation.

Yet, even if managers receive financial incentives to predate and firms hire managers who intrinsically value market share, how can predation be credible when the potential predator can be subject to a hostile takeover? Making credible commitments is profitable only if the firm does not have to carry out its threat. However, if entry occurs—despite a predatory firm's reputation for retaliation—, shareholders would want to renege on the firm's promise to predate. Simply promising to pay a manager so that he has an incentive to predate should the circumstance call for it or hiring a manager with the proper values is likely to be insufficient. Predatory threats may not deter new entry if, at the last moment before incurring losses, a firm either has the ability to alter the manager's compensation scheme or can replace him with someone who may not hold strong preferences to carry out the predatory commitment. And even if a predatory firm maintains both the current manager and his compensation scheme, a takeover could still force such changes.

Given that manager selection and compensation are necessary but not sufficient to make predation credible, firms must thus also make it difficult for themselves as well as for potential acquirers to change these arrangements. This can be done only if firms can commit not to alter incentives and can adopt rules which prevent a takeover. A more sophisticated model of predation might assume that potential predators hire managers who intrinsically value predation and are very difficult to fire. Firms may make it costly to fire managers by allowing large severance payments (golden parachutes). The greater the costs of firing a manager, the more likely that predators will fulfill their threats, despite the losses that they incur.

My discussion fits into an important literature that views management entrenchment devices as efficient because they prevent firms from opportunistically holding up managers (see Knoeber 1986).[4]

Firms may frequently find it efficient to compensate managers with a delay since the quality of projects that the managers initiate can only be evaluated later. However, this creates the problem that the firm has an incentive to remove the manager to save the cost of compensating him just when projects that he oversaw are coming to fruition. In terms of the game-theoretic predation literature, both the manager and the predatory firm can gain from the firm's credibly committing not to hold up the manager for the investment that he makes in the firm's reputation when predation becomes necessary.

Knoeber's argument also applies because managers of both predatory and nonpredatory firms make many similar types of investments that can be evaluated only with a lag. If predation increases the probability that the manager will lose his job, it implies that he may be opportunistically taken advantage of, and thus predatory firms should be more likely to have management entrenchment devices than other firms in the same industry. The first column in table 2.1 summarizes the predictions derived from the reputational predation theory.

B. The Length of the Time Horizon

The game-theoretic assumptions concerning the length of the time horizon or the number of potential entrants are crucial to understanding the preceding predictable implications.[5] For predation to ever be a rational strategy when the predator's time horizon is short or the number of potential entrants small, the probability that the incumbent is following a nonprofit-maximizing strategy must be relatively large. Conversely, as the time horizon or number of potential entrants approaches infinity, this probability can be quite small. This game-theoretic model also helps explain why it may pay for a firm to make initial investments in convincing other competitors that its managers value something other than profit maximization during early periods and then not be willing to make such investments toward the end of the time horizon. As the end of the time horizon approaches, it will not pay to create a reputation for predation. During the initial periods it can be worthwhile to create such a reputation, but this depends on the unraveling problem (or chain-store paradox problem) being solved through this reliance on preferences. For the intermediate periods predation will only continue because of commitments for nonprofit maximizing managers to respond to new entry. As the preceding discussion notes, these commitments cannot

Table 2.1   Predictions for managerial entrenchment and compensation during predation periods

	Predation theories				
	Reputation for toughness	Signaling false information		Long purse	Reputational model without last period
		Demand	Cost		
Managerial entrenchment important to ensuring strategies and "renegotiation proof"	YES If preferences are sufficient and we don't want to make it costly for manager to engage in predation Compensation if preferences are not sufficient to motivate manager	YES	NO	NO	(?)
Change in managerial compensation for "predatory" firms relative to nonpredatory ones based upon change in:					
Short-run profit	NEGATIVE OR NO RELATIONSHIP	NEGATIVE	POSITIVE	NEGATIVE	NEGATIVE
Sales	POSITIVE OR NO RELATIONSHIP	NEGATIVE	POSITIVE	POSITIVE	POSITIVE
Market value	POSITIVE OR NO RELATIONSHIP*	NEGATIVE	POSITIVE	(?)	POSITIVE

*This holds during the initial periods of the game. Toward the later periods the relationship between managerial compensation and market value becomes negative.

be made credible simply by hiring nonprofit maximizing managers, since these managers can be replaced unless restrictions exist to make their removal very costly.

Given that it pays for firms to make investments in reputation during the initial periods, there is no reason to expect these firms to differ initially from nonpredatory firms in terms of how costly it is to remove their managers. In that case, since predatory pricing is optimal and the board of directors and outside raiders realize this, price and short-term profits would fall, but there will be no turnover in management. It is only later that the firm might have an incentive to remove the aggressive manager rather than bear the short-run financial losses from predation. However, during the middle and end periods in the game, predatory firms will have a greater return to signaling entrants that potentially "tough" or "irrational" managers are not removed. In the empirical work that I examine later, it is not possible to distinguish which period of time a predatory firm is in. However, as long as the data contain some predatory firms from these later time periods, predatory firms will on average obtain a greater return to preventing managers from being removed than will nonpredatory firms. To the extent that my sample is dominated by firms that are only in the initial periods of predation, the less likely the sample will be to reveal any significant difference between predatory and nonpredatory firms.

While the models by Milgrom and Roberts as well as Kreps and Wilson assume that there is only some probability that a manager is irrational, I extend their discussion by pointing out that all firms deterring potential entry through the mechanism they describe will find it necessary to prevent managers from being easily removed. This is as true for firms without "irrational" managers as it is for those with them. If potential competitors observe that a predatory firm can easily remove its manager and that the predatory firm is in the middle or end period of the game, potential entrants will always enter.

C. Methods of Entrenching Management

While golden parachutes are one mechanism for protecting managers from removal, the practice of including them in management employment contracts did not arise until the late 1970s and they were not widely used until the early 1980s—since which time few predation cases have gone to court. Other mechanisms, however, could have been used to entrench management and thus shore up predatory threats. Firm characteristics identified in the literature as related to entrenchment include: (1) incorporation in a state which makes corporate takeovers difficult, (2) antitakeover charter amendments, (3) relatively large firm size, (4) a high fraction of shares held by management or the board of directors, (5) concentrated share ownership, (6) high R&D intensity, and (7) a high industry-adjusted Tobin's q. The remainder of this section reviews the evidence that these firm characteristics increase managerial entrenchment and thus help ensure costly predatory commitments.

There is little doubt that state takeover laws and antitakeover charter amendments increase the cost of hostile corporate acquisitions and entrench incumbent managers. Karpoff and Malatesta (1989) found substantial evidence that the initial press announcements of state takeover legislation resulted in small but statistically significant decreases in the equity market value of firms incorporated or headquartered in those states.[6] Potentially predatory firms, which would benefit from entrenching their management, should be found reincorporating in states that pass antitakeover legislation. I use firm size as a measure of entrenchment because buying large firms makes the buyer less diversified (Demsetz and Lehn 1985).[7] Research and development spending is also seen as a proxy for entrenchment since investments in research and development make it more costly to remove managers who have large specific human capital investments in evaluating research. It may be difficult for outsiders even to know what current research is, let alone infer the likelihood of success when products reach the market.[8]

The fraction of shares held by management, or possibly by the board of directors, should also increase management entrenchment (see Knoeber 1986). The larger this fraction, the greater is the proportion of the remaining shares which must be tendered for hostile takeovers to be successful. For similar reasons, if there are large shareholders who side with management, it will be more difficult to take over the firm.[9] Another proxy for management entrenchment is industry-adjusted Tobin's q—the ratio of the market value of a firm's liabilities to the book value of its assets relative to the industry average.[10] To the extent that poorly managed firms have a low q, then q provides a possible measure of the value created by a takeover.[11] So firms with a high q are less vulnerable to takeovers.

Barriers to management removal are generally costly, since they also protect inefficient management. Yet the ability to credibly follow through on predatory threats is necessary if the threats are going to be worthwhile in the first place. Instituting some types of entrenchment devices can be done at a low cost: for example, instituting an antitakeover charter amendment can be done fairly quickly and involves routine legal costs which are fairly low . Other entrenchment methods, such as increasing firm size, are much more costly. Nor is it necessary to assume that firms make new investments in order to predate. Instead, firms whose management happens to be more entrenched for some historical reasons may well also find it easier to engage in predation.

In general, however, one must be careful in interpreting the evidence provided later in section III showing that firms accused of predation neither provided accused predatory managers with additional protection from removal nor provided them with compensation that encourages predatory behavior. Two interpretations are possible: either that firms in my sample were, contrary to the charges, not engaging in predation; or, that if predation was occurring, it cannot be explained by theories which rely on firms hiring nonprofit maximizing managers.

D. The "Signaling" Literature

The discussion changes slightly when applied to the recent literature on signaling (Rasmusen 1991).[12] In the "signaling" model, the predatory firm conveys false information about industry demand or costs, leading potential entrants mistakenly to infer that they cannot profitably enter. When the predatory firm falsely signals that demand is low by competing "toughly," managers paid on the basis of stock value may not successfully be induced to act in the firm's long-run interest. Falsely signaling low demand can increase the present value of firm profits, yet if the stock market possesses the same incorrect information as potential entrants, the firm will temporarily lower its own stock value The manager then not only faces a temporary drop in income, but stockholders will be tempted to remove him from office. If a manager paid on the basis of stock value is to have the incentive to deceive his competitors, stockholders must not be able to remove him in the short run. The discussion is less complicated when firms deceive potential competitors into believing that the predator's costs are lower than they actually are. In that case, stock prices will rise, managers will be rewarded in the short term for conveying the incorrect information, and there is not the same type of hold-up problem.

Given that the signaling approach assumes that the predatory firm's managers know actual profitability, managers will rationally wish to purchase stock until its price reflects their knowledge. Tying managerial pay to the market value of equity will further induce managers to truthfully reveal their profitability from predation. This poses a dilemma for successful predation: if the stock price rises, it will make potential entrants question false signals that demand is low. There may be a free-rider problem where it would be in the interests of each individual member of a firm's management to purchase the stock and try to reap additional private profits. Ironically, this free-rider is prevented in the United States by insider trading laws, though firms could also write contracts with executives forbidding trading on inside information. Insider trading rules may then work to make predatory commitments more credible.

E. The "Long Purse" Literature

There exists another game-theoretic literature that should be noted, though I will not fully test this hypothesis in my book. Building upon Telser's notion of a predatory "advantage of having ample funds," Bolton and Scharfstein (1990) provide an incomplete-information model where a predation equilibrium arises because of agency problems and asymmetric information that the victim faces in the financial market. In their two-period model, predation does not have to change rivals' beliefs, but can adversely affect the prey's relationship to its creditors (p. 94). Creditors commit to terminate funding if a firm's performance is poor, creating an incentive for rivals to predate and damage the victim's financial position.[13] In this respect, the long purse model differs from the reputational models. The key for my discussion is that, as Ordover and Saloner (1989, 562) note, in a many-period setting "the long purse story must appeal to the reputation models for its explanation of why the incumbent is not faced with new entry when it attempts to raise its price post-exit. . . ." Because of this, their different approach to solving unraveling problems (or chain-store paradox problems) implies that reliance on preferences and its consequences for managerial entrenchment are not applicable to the long purse literature. However, the long purse story has straightforward implications for managerial compensation. If managers of predatory firms are to have the right incentives to expand output, their compensation during predatory periods must be more positively related to increased sales and more negatively related to lower profits than would be true for nonpredatory firms. The prediction for tying compensation to changes in market value is identical to the predictions made for the signaling literature. Assuming that the banks and the market have the same information, the direction of stock prices depends upon why they believe the victim is losing money. It is possible that the predatory firm's managerial compensation is either positively or negatively related to the firm's market value.

F. Reputational Models without Well-Defined Last Periods

Since the early 1980s, economists have developed many reputational models that do not rely upon managerial preferences. In these models, there is always some probability that the firm will be in existence, and thus the last period problem, with its unraveling consequences, never enters the picture (e.g., see particularly Klein and Leffler 1981 and for an application to these models of predation see Tirole 1990, 112 and 122–126).[14] Such a model of predation alters our preceding discussion on the length of the time horizon. For example, there is no longer the question of whether managers will be removed in the later periods of the game. Just as in the Milgrom and Roberts and the Kreps and Wilson models where the threat of removing managers is not a problem during the initial periods, where it can pay for firms to lose money in their quests to create reputations for toughness, these reputational models where there are no last periods essentially make all periods early periods in the game.

However, even though this new assumption no longer allows us to draw a prediction between predation and managerial entrenchment, predatory firms will still want to give managers the financial incentives to act in accordance with the firms' objectives. Thus I still do not expect predatory firms to link managerial compensation more closely with short-run profits or to reduce compensation when managers increase output during predatory periods.

III. Empirical Results

After describing the data, I will present evidence on (1) whether managerial compensation is consistent with managers of accused predatory firms being willing to engage in predation and (2) whether accused predatory firms displayed characteristics that entrenched management.

A. The Data

To investigate managerial compensation and entrenchment for firms accused of predatory pricing, I used a sample collected by Liebeler (1986) and Austin (1990) detailing court cases where a firm was sued for predatory pricing. Their studies list all 38 cases alleging predatory pricing that went to the appellate level between 1963 and 1988 and includes 18 additional district court cases that were not appealed.[15] Twenty-one of the defendant firms were both publicly traded and also reported in the COMPUSTAT data set.[16] Table 2.2 lists the defendant, plaintiff, appellate decision, the circuit or district court, and decision date, with a brief description of the allegations in each of these 21 cases involving a total of 28 firms. While I was unable to obtain time series information on the prices that alleged predatory firms charged before and after the predatory periods, table 2.2 indicates whether the court accepted the claim that the accused firm's price declined during the alleged predatory period. All the predatory acts were alleged to have occurred between 1958 and 1981, and lasted an average of 3.15 years. Predation was the primary allegation in most of these cases.

A second list of firms was constructed from district court data using Lexis. This was obtained from the district court sub-library using the phrase "predatory pricing" for the period between 1963 and 1988. A total of 29 cases dealt with predation charges that were not included in the Liebeler and Austin sample cases.[17] Of these cases, 12 involved publicly traded firms, and all 12 involved district courts issuing summary judgments for the defendant. While I conducted empirical tests using the appeals and district court data, I emphasize only the regressions using the Liebeler and Austin court data since the remaining district court observations represent particularly weak accusations of predation. Liebeler does include two cases involving summary dismissal (because they dealt with "some unique legal point" (p. 1061)), but removing them does not affect the results.

One concern with my sample arises from the inclusion of six cases heard by the Ninth Circuit. While all the other circuit courts have relied on cost tests to varying degrees, "[t]he Ninth Circuit has adopted an ultimate noncost standard under which a price should be considered predatory 'if its anticipated benefits depended on its tendency to eliminate competition'" (Austin 1990, 905; see also Gifford 1986). Because of the Ninth Circuit's different standards, I will also test how the results are affected by including these six cases. In

Table 2.2 Cases where predatory pricing was alleged: defendant, plaintiff, decision, decision date, court, and matter

Defendant(s)	Plaintiff	Years Alleged	Decision/Year/ Appeals court district	Matter / Did court accept claim that the accused firm's price declined during the alleged predatory period?
Champion Spark Plug	Stitt Spark Plug	1979–81	Defendant/1988/5th	Champion charged lower prices to industrial users because of their hold over the consumer market / No
Procter & Gamble	Indian Coffee	1973–74	Plaintiff/1980/3rd	Folgers gave discount coupons in Pennsylvania / Yes
Airco	Airweld	1969–76	Defendant/1985/4th	Airco entered market and charged predatory prices / Question not applicable, Airco just entered market.
Dr. Pepper	Bayou Bottling	1975	Defendant/1984/5th	Restraint of trade, contract dispute, and pricing below average variable costs / Yes
IBM	Transamerica Computer*	1970–78	Defendant/1983/9th	IBM lowered prices and changed its peripherals / Yes
MCA, ABC Records, Polygram Distribution, Warner/ Elektra/Atlantic, Capitol Records	Marin Music Centre	1969–75	Defendant/1982/9th	MCA & others sold records to chains at lower prices than independent retailer / No
Coca-Cola	Allegheny Pepsi-Cola Bottling	1979–80	Defendant/1982/4th	Parent company transferred "war chest" funds to subsidiary, allowing it to engage in predatory pricing / Yes
CPC International	Dimmitt Agri Industries	1970–73	Defendant/1982/5th	Below-cost prices by CPC in wet corn milling? / Yes

(continued)

Table 2.2 (continued)

Defendant(s)	Plaintiff	Years Alleged	Decision/Year/ Appeals court district	Matter / Did court accept claim that the accused firm's price declined during the alleged predatory period?
Borden	Golden Crown	1969–71	Plaintiff/1982/6th	Promotional pricing of ReaLemon juice / Yes
Monsanto	SuperTurf	1976–77	Defendant/1981/8th	Monsanto lowered price on AstroTurf / Yes
ITT	William Inglis Baking*	1971–74	Plaintiff/1980/9th	Continental set low prices on private label bread / Yes
United Brands	Pierce Packing	1972–75	Defendant/1980/9th	Sale of pork products below cost / Yes
Martin Marietta	Chillicothe Sand & Gravel	1973–78	Defendant/1980/7th	Martin Marietta sold gravel cheaply / Yes
Kerr-McGee	Pacific Engineering	1966–70	Defendant/1977/10th	Price cutting on solid fuel input for missiles / Yes
Shell Oil, Gulf Oil, Standard Oil	C. O. Hanson	1958–66	Defendant/1976/9th	Hanson claims was victimized in retail gas price wars in Tucson, AZ / Yes
Pepsico	Jays Foods	1974–80	Plaintiff/1985/7th	Frito Lay used promotional prices and ads to gain shelf space / Yes
Textron	Flair Zipper	1978–79	Defendant/1981/SDNY	Price reduction in New York zipper assembly market / Yes
Murphy Oil	Inter City Oil	1974–75	Defendant/1976/Minn.	Selling home heating oil below cost / Yes
Raytheon	CVD	1980–81	Plaintiff/1985/1st	Dispute over whether CVD should pay royalty rate on manufacture of zinc sulfide and zinc selenide / No
North American Phillips	Energex Lighting	1979–80	Plaintiff/1987/SDNY	Phillips set low prices to distributors, ignored Energex / Yes
Marathon Oil, Tenneco Oil	Spar Oil	1971–72	Plaintiff/1981/5th	Set price below Spar's gas station costs in south Georgia / Yes

NOTE: The complete legal citations for these cases are in Liebeler 1986 and Austin 1990.

*Three other predation cases were brought against IBM (two other 9th circuit and one 10th circuit) and one more against ITT (1st circuit) during the same time period.

general, I find that either there are no differences between the Ninth and other circuit courts, or that when differences do arise, the Ninth Circuit Court's decisions are most likely to punish innocent firms.

Data on the sales, R&D expenditures, operating income, firm employment, market value, and asset value of the publicly traded predation defendants were obtained from Standard and Poor's COMPUSTAT II Primary/Secondary/Tertiary, FC and Research Files. When available, market share data were obtained directly from the district or appeals court decisions. Alternatively, when those court decisions did not state market share, the COMPUSTAT sales data were employed to proxy for a firm's market share. The Forbes surveys from 1970 to 1989 on compensation data were used in order to analyze the sensitivity of compensation to performance, as well as to identify chief executive officers' turnover rates.[18] Their compensation data set for 683 firms over a total of 9,158 CEO-years of data includes: salary, bonuses, value of restricted stock grants, savings and thrift plans, and benefits. After 1978, total compensation also includes gains from stock options exercised (though not those granted) during the previous year.[19] Firms in the COMPUSTAT data set with an antitakeover charter amendment were identified by means of the data in DeAngelo and Rice (1983). I also determined whether firms were chartered in states with laws inhibiting hostile takeovers up until the 1982 *Edgar v. Mite* decision, which invalidated state antitakeover laws.[20] The concentration of share holdings for managers and outsiders with large holdings relies on the same data as those analyzed by Demsetz and Lehn (1985). All variables and their sources are listed in table 2.3.

I recognize that courts face many difficulties in evaluating whether predation has occurred and that they may be biased toward finding predation when none exists (Easterbrook 1984 and 1986). One important bias may be that judges tend to disapprove of efficiency explanations that they do not understand or are not persuaded by (Easterbrook 1984, 4–14). In addition, the data are derived from privately initiated suits. Since people tend to sue only when the expected gains exceed costs, and settle out of court when the outcome of a court case seems certain, these lawsuits undoubtedly do not represent the cases with the highest presumption that predation occurred (Priest and Klein 1984 and Wittman 1985).[21] In other words, relative to the group of cases where predation "truly" took place in the legal sense, I have a sample where there is less presumption that predation occurred. This does not affect my results much, though:

Table 2.3 Exogenous variables and their sources

Variable name	Description and source
PREDATION FIRM	Dummy variable equaling one if the firm was charged with having engaged in predation during 1963–1988 (Source: Liebeler 1986 and Austin 1990)
PREDATION YEAR	Dummy variable equaling one if the firm was accused of having engaged in predation during a particular year (Source: Liebeler 1986 and Austin 1990)
CONVICTED AND PRICE DROP FIRM	Dummy variable equaling one if the firm was convicted of having engaged in predation and the court found evidence of a price drop during 1963–1988 (Source: Liebeler 1986, Austin 1990, and the individual district and appeals court decisions)
CONVICTED AND PRICE DROP YEAR	Dummy variable equaling one if the firm was convicted of having engaged in predation and the court found evidence of a price drop during a particular year (Source: Liebeler 1986, Austin 1990, and the individual district and appeals court decisions)
PROFIT GROWTH	The difference between the current year's operating income to sales and the previous year's operating income to sales divided by the firm's operating income to sales in the previous year (Source: COMPUSTAT)
SALES GROWTH	The difference between the current year's sales revenues and the previous year's sales revenues divided by the firm's sales revenues in the previous year (Source: COMPUSTAT)
MARKET VALUE GROWTH	The difference between the current year's market value of equity and the preceding year's value divided by the firm's market value of equity in the previous year (Source: COMPUSTAT)
INDUSTRY-ADJUSTED TOBIN'S Q	The market value of equity plus the book values of debt and preferred stock all divided by the book value of a firm's assets adjusted for inflation by the producer price index (Source: COMPUSTAT)
R&D INTENSITY	R&D divided by sales (Source: COMPUSTAT)
Fraction of shares held by the top 4 owners	The percentage of a firm's stock held by its four largest shareholders (Source: Demsetz and Lehn 1985)
ANTITAKEOVER CHARTER AMENDMENTS	A dummy variable that equaled one for identified firms in the COMPUSTAT data set which had antitakeover charter amendments (Source: DeAngelo and Rice 1983)

Table 2.3   (continued)

Variable name	Description and source
ANTITAKEOVER LAW	A dummy variable that equaled one for firms chartered in states with laws inhibiting hostile takeovers up until the 1982 *Edgar v. Mite* decision which invalidated state antitakeover laws (Source: Karpoff and Malatesta 1989)
MANAGER TURNOVER RATE	The annualize average rate at which chief executive officers lose their positions during the sample period (Source: *Forbes* magazine, 1970–1989)
ANNUAL MANAGERIAL TURNOVER RATE	A variable that equals one if there was a turnover during a given year (Source: *Forbes* magazine, 1970–1989)
CEO COMPENSATION	Salary, bonuses, value of restricted stock grants, savings and thrift plans, and benefits (Source: *Forbes* magazine, 1970–1989)
CEO AGE	(Source: *Forbes* magazine, 1970–1989)
Other variables on Firm Assets, Sales, and Employment	(Source: COMPUSTAT)

even if many obviously guilty firms settle, we can still presume that the set of firms charged contains a greater percentage of guilty firms than does the comparison group of firms not charged with predation. To believe that the probabilities of guilt are the same or greater for the comparison sample than for those firms actually charged or convicted implies that the legal system is either random or perverse, which would thus challenge whether there should even be *any* penalties for predation.

There is also the question about why competitors enter against those firms that are committed to engage in predation. Presumably, entry occurs either because entrants are making a mistake or because the incumbent firm has not done enough to entrench managers or provide them with the proper incentives to lower price and expand output. If at least some entry results from mistakes being made by entrants, the predatory and nonpredatory firms will, on average, exhibit the differences in characteristics that I predict. Alternatively, if entry is arising only because predators have not made sufficient investments to convince potential entrants that they will follow through on their threats, presumably the predators have at least made a larger investment than nonpredatory firms in encouraging managers to increase output and decrease short-term profits as well as in entrenching managers.

A couple of caveats should be mentioned. The power of the tests presented in this chapter is limited by the size of the sample: it is small because few firms have been accused or convicted of predation and because management compensation is available for only a subset of these firms. Nonetheless, these tests provide the first systematic evidence on whether the firms suspected of predation behave in accordance with the reputational models for tough managers. The tests also provide evidence as to whether firms encouraged their managers to engage in predation through their compensation schemes. Limiting the sample to publicly traded firms also prevents us from drawing conclusions about how these game-theoretic models apply to privately held firms (see also Hansen and Lott 1995). Since, as I noted earlier, privately held firms should be best able to prevent takeover threats, the evidence on privately held firms might be more likely to support these models. However, because of their usually smaller size they are less likely to be predatory threats.

B. Did Firms Increase Sales and Decrease Profits during Predatory Periods?

Before we proceed with the more rigorous tests outlined in section II, a couple of simple regressions can provide some rough evidence for whether the correct firms were being punished. If a firm is engaging in predatory action (even if it is with the notion of creating a reputation for toughness), its output should increase and profits fall. To examine this, I pooled together two types of cross-sectional and time-series evidence for the firms shown in table 2.2, using the 1956–1985 sample from the COMPUSTAT data set. I regressed the sales growth rate (the difference in sales between years one and two divided by sales in year one) for all firms in the COMPUSTAT panel on a dummy variable indicating whether the firm was accused (PRE-DATION YEAR) of having engaged in predation during a particular year. Another dummy variable measuring whether firms were convicted during a particular year only equals one when the courts also found evidence of a price drop (CONVICTED AND PRICE DROP YEAR). In an attempt to control for changing industry fortunes, I also included a third variable that controls for each industry's yearly average percent change in sales. The second regression examines the change in firm profits in a similar manner. I obtained the following results:

Sales Growth = −.0067 Predation Year
           (0.101)
           + .0237 Convicted and Price Drop Year
           (0.209)
           + 1.00 Industry Yearly Average Sales Growth   (1)
           (52.437)
           − 1.09E − 5
           (0.002)
    N = 8009   F-statistic = 916.55   adj-R^2 = .2554

Profit Growth = −.011 Predation Year
           (0.218)
           + .009 Convicted and Price Drop Year
           (0.104)
           + 1.00 Industry Yearly Average Profit Growth   (2)
           (91.74)
           + 5.69E − 5
           (0.016)
    N = 7929   F-statistic = 2805.5   adj-R^2 = .5148,

where the absolute t-statistics are shown in parentheses.[22] To determine the change in sales or profits for convicted firms that lowered their prices, it is necessary to add the coefficients from accused and convicted firms together since all convicted firms are obviously also classified as being accused. The regressions indicate that firms that were both convicted of predation and experienced price drops increased sales and decreased profits, though none of the coefficients measuring predation is statistically significant. The net effects for firms that were both convicted and experienced price drops were also very small, implying a sales increase by 1.7 percent and a profits decrease by 0.2 percent. In comparison, a one standard deviation in the percent change in sales is 47 percent, and in profits 45 percent.

While the point estimates for convicted firms are consistent with predatory behavior, the evidence implies that the firms which both were convicted and experienced price drops behaved essentially the same as other firms. The results remained virtually identical when these predation dummies were replaced with dummy variables that equaled one only during the first year that the sample firms were accused or convicted of predation, when the dummy variable Convicted and Price Drop Year is replaced with a dummy variable measuring only whether a firm has been convicted of predation, when the Log of sales is included to measure firm size, or when only the dummy variables for PREDATION YEAR and CONVICTED AND PRICE DROP YEAR are used.

C. Compensation, Predation, and Performance

As emphasized earlier, credible predation requires that management compensation contracts reward market share expansion rather than short-term profitability in periods of entry. Predatory firms are also likely to have greater returns than other firms from aligning managers' interests with shareholders' long-term interests through tying managerial compensation to the value of the firm's stock. Managers need to persuade entrants that they are likely to be market share maximizers and that the firms will reward them for these actions.[23]

Table 2.4 briefly describes the incentive compensation offered executives during the period when predation was alleged, and then compares them to those in competing, similarly sized firms not charged with predation.[24] The information in the table was compiled from the financial footnotes in annual reports and U.S. Securities and Exchange Commission 10-K filings and proxy statements. While the initial comparisons are quite rough since compensation based upon options and profits is subject to many restrictions, the table indicates no obvious differences between the two sets of firms. Managers of nonpredatory firms receive salaries that are only slightly more based on their firm's short-term profits and slightly less on options. While both differences are consistent with credible predatory commitments, the numbers for predatory and nonpredatory firms are virtually identical—simply switching one-tenth of one firm in the options category and one-seventh of one firm in the profits columns is enough to eliminate any differences between predatory and nonpredatory firms. Nor are the differences statistically significant: a t-test on the differences in means for the options dummy variable provides a $t = 0.07$ (p - value $= 0.94$) and for the profit dummy variable a $t = 0.05$ (p - value $= .96$).

Whether firms accused of predatory actions were more or less likely to base managerial compensation upon options or short-term profits can be examined more systematically by using logit regressions. To do this, I regressed an options dummy variable that equaled one whenever managerial compensation included options on a dummy variable for whether a firm was accused of predation (PREDATION FIRM) and a variable that measuring the average rate at which

Table 2.4 Description of manager compensation contract in period of alleged predatory pricing

Defendant	Options	Profits	Other	Comparison I	Options	Profits	Other	Comparison II	Options	Profits	Other
Dr. Pepper	Yes	Yes	B	Norton Simon (Canada Dry)	Yes	No	G				
Coca-Cola	Yes	No		Consol. Foods (Shasta)	Yes	Yes	J				
Pepsico	No	Yes		IC Industries (Pepsi Bottlers)	Yes	No					
Marathon Oil	Yes	Yes		Exxon	Yes	Yes		American Petrofina	Yes	No	
Shell Oil	Yes	Yes		Mobil	Yes	Yes		Superior Oil	Yes	No	
Gulf Oil	Yes	Yes	I	Texaco	Yes	No		Getty Oil	No	No	F
Standard Oil	Yes	No		Phillips Pet.	No	No	K	Amoco	Yes	Yes	
Murphy Oil	Yes	No	I	ARCO	Yes	No	C	Gulf Oil	Yes	No	
Champion Spark Plug	Yes	Yes	F	Eltra	Yes	No		General Motors (AC Delco)	Yes	Yes	
Procter & Gamble	Yes	No	A	Standard Brands	Yes	Yes	A,E	General Foods	Yes	No	
Airco	No	Yes		Union Carbide	Yes	Yes		Air Prods. & Chems.	Yes	Yes	
IBM	Yes	Yes	I	Sperry Rand	Yes	Yes		Burroughs	Yes	No	L
MCA	Yes	No	C	CBS	Yes	Yes		RCA	Yes	Yes	H
Warner Communications	Yes	No		ABC	Yes	No		Columbia	Yes	No	
Capital Industries	Yes	Yes		MGM	Yes	No		Gulf + Western	Yes	No	
CPC International	Yes	Yes		A.E. Staley	Yes	No		Standard Brands	Yes	Yes	A,E
Borden	Yes	No		Beatrice	Yes	No		Carnation	Yes	Yes	

(continued)

Table 2.4 (continued)

Defendant	Options	Profits	Other	Comparison I	Options	Profits	Other	Comparison II	Options	Profits	Other
Monsanto	Yes	No		E. I. Dupont	Yes	Yes		Celanese	Yes	No	
ITT	Yes	No	I	Amer. Bakeries	Yes	Yes		Ward Foods	Yes	No	A
United Brands	Yes	No		Iowa Beef Proc.	Yes	No		Esmark	Yes	No	
Martin Marietta	Yes	No		Vulcan Materials	No	Yes	F,E	Florida Rock	No	Yes	F
Kerr-McGee	Yes	No		American Cyanimid	Yes	No		Allied Chemical	Yes	Yes	
Textron	Yes	No		Levi Strauss	Yes	Yes	E	West Point Pepperell	Yes	Yes	E
Raytheon	Yes	Yes		McDonnell Douglas	Yes	Yes		Lockheed	Yes	No	
North American Phillips	Yes	No		Natl. Service Industries	Yes	No		General Electric	Yes	No	
Frequency of plan type	92%	44%						Comparison I and II	91.5%	44.7%	

A. Shares must be sold back to company when terminated.

B. Formula based on return relative to investment.

C. Executives guaranteed jobs in contracts.

E. No share or cash bonuses paid unless earnings growth exceeds threshold.

F. High stock ownership by executives.

G. Cash bonus awards tied to stock price growth.

H. Bonus pool tied to dividends.

I. Basis for distributing bonuses not specified.

J. Compensation triggered when earnings growth and return on investment targets met.

K. Option program terminated in 1963.

L. Stock options given when earnings target met.

the firms in each 2-digit industry classification use options. A similar logit regression was run using the information on compensation based on short-term profits.

Options = 0.079 Predation Firm
        (0.099)
        + 10.729 Industry Average Rate for Options − 6.769   (3)
          (2.890)   (2.269)
                Log Likelihood = −15.642

Profits = −0.05287 Predation Firm
         (0.098)
         + 5.042 Industry Avg. Rate for Using Short-term Profits
           (2.969)   (4)
         − 2.447
           (3.036)
                Log Likelihood = −43.457

Chi-squared statistics are shown in parentheses. Including another dummy variable for whether the firm was convicted and whether there was a price drop also produced chi-squared values that were less than 0.2 for both predation dummies. At least for this extremely rough first look at the data, these results confirm that firms accused of predation do not appear to base executive compensation on options or short-term profits any differently than firms that are not accused.

Obviously, however, management compensation frequently involves implicit agreements, and, even when they are explicit, firms often do not make all the rules publicly available. Previous authors (e.g., Murphy 1985) have, nonetheless, examined compensation contracts by empirically regressing changes in total management pay on changes in firm performance. I also adopt this approach to determine whether managers of firms in the sample had compensation contracts (implicit or explicit) that rewarded predatory behavior.

I estimate a set of linear regressions over 437 firms to predict the percentage change in total executive pay. The independent variables in these regressions include growth in profit, growth in sales revenues, and growth in the market value of equity. The growth variables are simply the current year's values divided by those from the previous year. A vector of compensation shifters, which are suggested by previous studies, is also included. These are the chief executive officer's age, that age squared, industry dummies, year dummies, and proxies for firm size measured by the log of sales and the log of assets.[25]

The independent variables of greatest interest here are: interactions of growth in sales, market value, and profits with dummy variables for firms accused of predation. Firms accused of predation are identified in four ways: (1) with a dummy variable (PREDATION FIRM) which indicates whether they were ever sued for predation in cases that went to the appellate level between 1963 and 1985, (2) a dummy variable (PREDATION YEAR) that shows the years of alleged predation, (3) a dummy variable (CONVICTED AND PRICE DROP FIRM) that indicates the firms *convicted* of predation and where the court also concluded that the price had fallen during the predatory period, and (4) a dummy variable (CONVICTED AND PRICE DROP YEAR) that indicates years of alleged predation only for firms *convicted* of predation and where price had fallen. The coefficients on these interaction variables measure the incremental importance of a given operating performance measure in determining growth in executive pay.

If firms want to encourage managers to predate, the regressions should show a significant negative coefficient on growth in profits multiplied by the predation dummy and a significant positive coefficient on sales growth multiplied by the predation dummy. Table 2.5 shows several regressions including these coefficients for the firms in the sample. The first specification focuses on whether there are any significant differences between predatory and nonpredatory firms. While the positive coefficient on the SALES GROWTH × PREDATION FIRM is consistent with the reputational theory of predation and the positive coefficient on the PROFIT GROWTH × PREDATION FIRM is not, only the profit growth interaction is statistically significant. The PROFIT GROWTH × PREDATION FIRM is also economically large, implying that predatory firms increase executive compensation five times faster than nonpredatory firms when short-term profits increase. For predatory firms, decreasing short-term profits reduces net executive compensation by about 10 times more than does the same percentage drop in sales. This significant positive coefficient for PROFIT GROWTH × PREDATION FIRM is inconsistent with the predation theories based upon a reputation for toughness.

The second specification also answers whether these effects were different during the reported periods of predation using variables for SALES GROWTH × PREDATION YEAR, PROFIT GROWTH × PREDATION YEAR, and MARKET VALUE GROWTH × PREDATION YEAR. These variables identify sample firms in the years they allegedly predated.

Table 2.5 Regressions of annual growth rate in management compensation versus profit, sales, and market value growth and predation interaction terms during 1970–1985

	(1)	(2)	(3)	(4)	(5)	(6)	(7)
Intercept	0.696 (1.71)	0.730 (1.79)	0.695 (1.71)	0.728 (1.79)	0.729 (1.79)	0.730 (1.79)	0.683 (1.68)
Profit growth	0.080 (6.04)	0.082 (6.16)	0.081 (6.05)	0.083 (6.22)	0.083 (6.23)	0.083 (6.22)	0.080 (6.04)
Sales growth	−0.047 (4.05)	−0.048 (4.18)	−0.047 (4.05)	−0.049 (4.21)	−0.049 (4.20)	−0.049 (4.20)	−0.047 (4.05)
Market Value growth	0.122 (7.75)	0.126 (8.02)	0.122 (7.75)	0.127 (8.06)	0.126 (8.02)	0.126 (8.03)	0.123 (7.75)
Profit growth x predation firm dummy	0.406 (2.62)	—	0.393 (2.19)	—	—	—	0.465 (2.11)
Sales growth x predation firm dummy	0.105 (0.48)	—	0.177 (0.65)	—	—	—	0.437 (1.15)
Market Value growth x predation firm dummy	0.055 (0.78)	—	0.090 (1.00)	—	—	—	0.093 (0.87)
Profit growth x predation year dummy	—	0.393 (1.26)	0.003 (0.01)	—	—	—	−0.092 (0.23)
Sales growth x predation year dummy	—	−0.052 (0.14)	−0.219 (0.47)	—	—	—	.422 (0.77)
Market Value growth x predation year dummy	—	−0.029 (0.24)	−0.117 (0.78)	—	—	—	0.09 (0.87)
Profit growth x convicted and price drop from dummy	—	—	—	0.554 (1.39)	—	1.032 (1.878)	1.105 (1.898)
Sales growth x convicted and price drop firm dummy	—	—	—	−0.955 (0.66)	—	−0.860 (0.48)	−0.435 (0.27)

(continued)

Table 2.5 (continued)

	(1)	(2)	(3)	(4)	(5)	(6)	(7)
Market Value growth x convicted and price drop firm dummy	—	—	—	0.020 (0.71)	—	-0.007 (0.02)	0.123 (0.33)
Profit gorwth x convicted and price drop year dummy	—	—	—	—	0.044 (1.41)	0.022 (0.07)	-0.48 (0.22)
Sales growth x convicted and price drop year dummy	—	—	—	—	-0.127 (0.34)	-0.094 (0.243)	-0.51 (0.95)
Market Value growth x convicted and price drop year dummy	—	—	—	—	0.018 (0.13)	0.027 (0.16)	-0.064 (0.32)
CEO age	0.0056 (0.86)	0.0050 (0.78)	0.006 (0.87)	0.0051 (0.80)	0.0053 (0.83)	0.0051 (0.80)	0.006 (0.93)
CEO age squared	$-6.5E{-}5$ (1.15)	$-6.0E{-}5$ (1.07)	$-6.5E{-}5$ (1.15)	$-6.1E{-}5$ (1.07)	$-6.2E{-}5$ (1.08)	$-6.1E{-}5$ (1.08)	$-6.9E{-}5$ (1.21)
Total assets	$-7.3E{-}5$ (1.39)	$-7.8E{-}5$ (1.47)	$-7.3E{-}5$ (1.49)	$-7.9E{-}5$ (1.49)	$-7.9E{-}5$ (1.50)	$-7.9E{-}5$ (1.50)	$-7.4E{-}5$ (1.41)
Log of sales	0.032 (2.70)	0.034 (2.92)	0.032 (2.66)	0.035 (2.94)	0.035 (2.94)	0.035 (2.95)	0.032 (2.67)
Log of employment	-0.030 (2.86)	-0.032 (3.07)	-0.030 (2.82)	-0.032 (3.06)	-0.032 (3.07)	-0.032 (3.07)	-0.30 (2.82)
Observations	7514	7514	7514	7514	7514	7514	7514
Adjusted R^2	0.062	0.061	0.062	0.060	0.061	0.060	0.062

NOTE: Convicted firm-years represent periods when a firm was alleged to have engaged in predation and was convicted at the appellate court level. Price decline firm-years represent periods when a firm was alleged to have engaged in predation and court documents confirm that a product price decline took place. Year and industry dummies are not shown. Management compensation equals base pay plus bonus.

Again, the results contradict the predation hypothesis. Managers of firms accused of predation were rewarded *more* for increasing short-term profits in predation years than were other managers, and the effect is economically large—larger in fact than the direct effect of profit growth, though the coefficient is statistically insignificant. For example, if a firm accused of predation decreased profits by 10 percent when predation was supposedly occurring, managerial compensation fell by 3.9 percent. The point estimates even imply that managers were *penalized* for increasing sales during years that they were accused of engaging in predation, though the coefficient on SALES GROWTH × PREDATION YEAR is statistically insignificant. This pattern of coefficients is not consistent with the reputational theory of predation.[26]

The third specification combines the dummy variables employed in the first two specifications so that it is possible to differentiate between predatory firms and how those firms' behavior changed during the years that the alleged violations occurred. The results are almost identical to the earlier ones. Only the PROFIT GROWTH × PREDATION YEAR variable is significant, and it shows that alleged predators actually decrease their managers' compensation by 3.9 percent for every 10 percent decrease in profits. The coefficients for SALES GROWTH × PREDATION FIRM and SALES GROWTH × PREDATION YEAR are still insignificant, and the net effect is negative, though economically quite small—increasing sales by 10 percent reduces the managerial compensation in accused firms by only 0.42 percent more than it does for other firms.

Specifications 4, 5, and 6 allow us to check if firms convicted of predatory pricing compensated their managers differently in the years that the predation allegedly occurred. Firms convicted of predation and whose prices fell during the alleged predatory period showed a greater propensity to compensate their managers on the basis of accounting profits than did other firms. The point estimates were larger than those shown in the previous columns, though the variables were statistically significant in only two of the three cases. In addition, I find negative, but statistically insignificant, coefficients on SALES GROWTH × CONVICTED AND PRICE DROP YEAR and SALES GROWTH × CONVICTED AND PRICE DROP FIRM. However, while statistically insignificant, the coefficients are quite large—9 to 19 times larger than the direct effect of sales growth on managerial compensation. Again, both the profit and sales growth results are at odds with the notion that firms are encouraging managers to engage in predation. The measures dealing with stock returns imply that differences for predatory firms are both economically small and statistically insignificant.

Reestimating the regressions in table 2.5 using only two measures of firm performance at a time (i.e., SALES GROWTH and MARKET VALUE GROWTH, PROFIT GROWTH and MARKET VALUE GROWTH, and PROFIT GROWTH and SALES GROWTH) produces results that are even more frequently the opposite signs and significant from what is predicted by the reputational predatory theory.

I also broke down the specifications in table 2.5 according to how accused or convicted firms behaved during the first year of alleged predation, as well as whether the Ninth Circuit Court cases differed from those in the other circuits. While respecifying the regressions so that the dummy variables CONVICTED AND PRICE DROP YEAR and PREDATION YEAR were replaced by FIRST CONVICTED AND PRICE DROP YEAR and FIRST PREDATION YEAR did not alter the results, eliminating the six Ninth Circuit Court cases caused all the CONVICTED AND PRICE DROP FIRM and PREDATION FIRM coefficients to be insignificant. While these last results still fail to support the reputational theory of predation, they suggest that the Ninth Circuit's decisions involved a set of cases that were particularly inconsistent with predatory theory. Specifically, the results show that managers of firms taken before the Ninth Circuit were paid more when they increased profits during supposedly predatory periods.

While one expects that managerial compensation must increase when profits decline if managers are to have the correct incentives to engage in predation, managerial compensation should be even less positively related to profits for those firms where predation is occurring in their primary product line. The coefficients on the predation dummy variables would thus be more likely to have the predicted signs if the empirical work examined only those firms which were accused of engaging in predation with their primary output. To test this possibility, I reran the specifications shown in table 2.5, but included only firms where predation involved their primary output. I chose six companies for these new regressions: the oil companies (Marathon, Shell, and Murphy), two of the soft drink companies (Coca-Cola and Dr. Pepper), and an automotive parts company (Champion Spark Plug). The results are again very similar to those previously reported.

Table 2.6 reports the third specification used in table 2.5 but by

Table 2.6 Industry-level regressions of change in compensation on determinants of compensation with interactions for firms accused of predation

Variable	Chemicals (SIC = 28)		Electronics (SIC = 36)		Food (SIC = 20)		Petroleum (SIC = 29)	
	Coeff	t-stat	Coeff	t-stat	Coeff	t-stat	Coeff	t-stat
Intercept	-0.746	-0.72	-0.986	-0.52	0.088	0.12	-0.146	-0.15
Profit growth	0.491	5.21	-0.011	-0.16	0.131	1.26	0.149	1.31
Sales growth	-0.151	-0.87	0.314	1.37	-0.109	-0.68	0.237	1.24
Market Value growth	0.208	3.00	0.250	1.02	0.112	1.33	0.129	1.32
Profit growth × predation year	0.014	0.01	-1.15	-0.46	0.240	0.16	-0.083	-0.17
Sales growth × predation year	-1.39	-0.46	-0.028	-0.01	-0.091	-0.05	-0.519	-0.40
Market Value growth × predation year	0.401	0.43	-0.460	-1.16	-0.054	-0.12	-0.083	-0.17
Profit growth × predation firm	-0.043	-0.08	0.600	1.24	-0.293	-0.42	-0.539	-1.12
Sales growth × predation firm	0.305	0.29	0.134	0.19	0.534	0.67	0.221	0.42
Market Value growth × predation firm	-0.175	-0.61	0.250	1.02	0.186	0.85	-0.021	-0.09
CEO age	0.031	0.86	0.047	0.69	-0.003	-0.12	0.017	0.54
CEO age squared	-2.9E-4	-0.90	-4.1E-4	-0.68	2.3E-5	0.10	-1.7E-4	-0.66
Total assets	3.8E-4	-0.90	7.2E-5	0.08	-5.3E-4	-0.40	1.2E-4	0.41
Log of sales	0.004	0.06	0.027	0.30	0.069	1.51	-0.023	-0.41
Log of employees	0.007	0.15	-0.036	-0.47	-0.027	-0.88	0.021	0.44
Observations	685		292		424		295	
Adjusted R^2	0.11		0.11		0.01		0.10	

2-digit SIC industry classification. (The other specifications were tried and produced similar results.) The industry regressions examine whether firms accused of predation differ from others in their primary 2-digit SIC industry. None of the 24 coefficients that interact predation firm or predation year dummies are statistically significant, suggesting that firms accused of predation do not differ from other firms in their compensation structure. In addition, no clear pattern stands out: nine of the twelve coefficients measuring the effects during the alleged predation and three of the twelve coefficients controlling for whether the firms were charged with predation have the opposite signs from what the predation theory predicts. Finding no systematic differences in pay structure between the two groups of firms makes it difficult to believe the reputational theory of predation.

Earlier I interpreted the negative coefficient on SALES GROWTH × PREDATION YEAR to imply that managers were not rewarded for increasing sales. However, given that this variable measures total revenues as opposed to the quantity of output, it is possible that managers were indeed rewarded for increasing output—despite the negative coefficient on SALES GROWTH × PREDATION YEAR—because revenue can fall as prices decline. Demand and supply elasticities of the products sold by the firms in the sample can be used to answer this question, though estimation of such elasticities is relatively imprecise. Table 2.7 reports the demand elasticities and market shares for product classes for the sample's firms. Yearly demand elasticities are used since all the sales data are on a yearly basis.

Table 2.7 indicates that four firms face elastic demand. For these firms, increases in revenues mean increased output. Thirteen other firms belong to industries with inelastic demands. For these firms, growth in sales does not necessarily imply increased output, since industry demand elasticities can greatly underestimate the true elasticity facing any individual firm. When a predatory firm reduces price, it must increase output not only to make up for the increased quantity demanded from the lower price, but also to make up for cutbacks by other firms in the industry. The greater the cutback by other firms due to the lower price, the greater is the effective demand elasticity facing the individual predatory firm. The last column of table 2.7 reports the supply elasticity required of other firms for the predatory firm to face a unitary elastic demand curve.[27] Even at very low supply elasticities, the predator faces elastic demands. In all but two cases, a supply elasticity as low as 0.43 causes the predatory firm to face an

Table 2.7 Estimated market shares and demand elasticities in industries where predatory pricing was alleged, with the industry supply elasticity values that are required for firm revenue coefficients to primarily reflect the impact of quantity changes

Defendant	SIC	SIC Industry	Market share at beginning of predatory period (%)	Industry	Demand Elasticity	The maximum industry supply elasticity which implies the coefficient on firm revenue still reflects quantity changes
Champion Spark Plug	3694	Automotive parts	50	Tires, tubes, parts	1.93[a]	<0
Procter & Camble	2095	Roasted coffee	0	Coffee	0.25[a]	0.75
Airco	2813	Industrial gases	0	N/A		
Dr. Pepper	2086	Soft drinks	2.9*	Soft drinks	0.90[b]	0.10
IBM	3573	Computer & office equipment	32.3*	N/A		
MCA	3652	Phonograph records	5.6*	Radio, TV, records	3.00[a]	< 0
Coca-Cola	2087	Soft drinks	39.3*	Soft drinks	0.90[b]	0.165
CPC International	2046	Wet corn milling	25	Food	0.71[a]	0.38
Borden	5141	Grocery products, general	10–90	Food	0.71[a]	0.32 to 2.9
Monsanto	2824	Manmade fiber	78	N/A		
ITT	2051	Bread & bakery products	17	Bread	0.06[c]	1.13
United Brands	2011	Meat packing plants	21	Beef	0.92[d]	0.10
Martin Marietta	1423	Crushed & broken limestone	70	N/A		
Kerr-McGee Corp	2865	Cyclic organic crudes	54	Gasoline	0.80[e]	0.43
Shell Oil, Standard Oil	5541	Gas stations	10	Gasoline	0.80[e]	0.22 for Combined Market Share: 0.25
			9			0.22
Pepsico	2099	Snack foods	25	Food	0.71[a]	0.38
Textron	3964	Needles, pins, fasteners	30.6*	Clothing	0.51[a]	0.70
Murphy Oil	1311	Petroleum extraction	25	Gasoline	0.80[e]	0.26
Raytheon	3761	Guided missile & space products	90	Optical material for high speed jet aircraft	1.69[f]	< 0

(continued)

Table 2.7 (continued)

Defendant	SIC	SIC Industry	Market share at beginning of predatory period (%)	Industry	Demand Elasticity	The maximum industry supply elasticity which implies the coefficient on firm revenue still reflects quantity changes
North American Phillips	3646	Commercial lighting fixtures	25	Electricity	1.94[a]	< 0
Marathon Oil, Tenneco	5541	Gas stations	<10	Gasoline	0.80[c]	0.22 for Combined Market Share: 0.25
Oil			<10			0.22

NOTE: Market shares were primarily obtained from either the district or appeals court decisions. When that information was not available we contacted the lawyers who represented the firms. We greatly appreciate the help of Ken Bode of Jenner & Block (Chicago) with the *Chillicothe v. Martin Marietta* case; Kenneth Letzler of Arnold & Porter (Washington, D.C.) for the *Allegheny Pepsi-Cola Bottling Co. v. Mid-Atlantic Coca-Cola Bottling Co.* case; Wayne Paris (Houston) and Rufus Oliver of Baker & Borts (Houston) with the *Stitt Spark Plug v. Champion Spark Plug Co.* case; Charles E. Buffon of Washington, D.C. for the *Flair Zipper Corp. v. Textron Inc.* case; Trammell Newton of Jones & Day (Atlanta) for the *Spar Oil Co. v. Marathon Oil Co. et al.* case; and Robert F. Finke of Mayer, Brown & Platt (Chicago) for the *Pierce Packing Co. v. John Morrell Co.* case.

*Market share estimate from COMPUSTAT data set.

***U.S. Congress, Senate, Select Committee on Nutrition and Human Needs, 1975 Food Price Study, Part IV: Economic Organization of the Milling and Bread Industry, 94th Congress, 1st Session, December 1975, pp. 56–61. This estimate is the only one that is not for the beginning of the alleged predatory period.

[a]From H. S. Houthakker and Lester D. Taylor, *Consumer Demand in the United States: Analyses and Projections* (Cambridge: Harvard University Press), 1970.

[b]From Noel D. Uri, "The Demand for Beverages and Interbeverage Substitution in the United States," *Bulletin of Economic Research* 38 (1986): 77–85.

[c]From Kenneth W. Meinken, *The Demand for and Price for Wheat*, Technical Bulletin No. 1136, U.S. Dept. of Agriculture, Washington, D.C., 1955.

[d]From Elmer Working, *The Demand for Meat* (Chicago: University of Chicago Press, 1951).

[e]From J. L. Sweeney, "The Response of Energy Demand to Higher Prices: What Have We Learned?" *American Economic Review* 74 (May 1984): 31–37.

[f]From Gerald S. McDougall and Dong W. Cho, "Demand Estimates for New General Aviation Aircraft: A User-cost Approach," *Applied Economics* 20 (1988): 315–324.

elastic demand. (The Borden case is the only case where there is a question of whether it is above or below this value.) The previous results reported in table 2.5 are not sensitive to which observations are excluded.[28] It does not matter whether the regressions drop out either the two firms whose required supply elasticities exceed 0.43, the one case where industry supply elasticities were clearly greater than one, or the thirteen firms where the maximum supply elasticities were greater than or equal to zero. In fact, the PROFIT GROWTH × PREDATION FIRM variable always continues to be positive and significant. These results suggest that sales revenue serves as a reasonable proxy for firm output in the sample.

In sum, the positive, large, and frequently statistically significant relationship between profits and compensation may simply reflect that firms that encourage managers to increase short-run profits are more likely to be accused of predation. The results provide strong evidence that accused firms are not rewarding managers for predatory behavior. The results are also at odds with all but one version of the signaling models. Yet, even when the short-run profit coefficients are consistent with the version of the signaling model illustrating that false information is being produced about a firm's demand curve, the other coefficients indicating how compensation is related to changes in sales and market value are frequently inconsistent. Over 80 percent of the time, the coefficients on sales growth were the opposite sign of what the predation theories predict, and the effect was often quite large, though never statistically significant.

D. Predation and Management Entrenchment

As well as testing whether managers charged with predation were compensated on the basis of sales, I have also tested whether managers accused of predation are more difficult to remove through hostile takeovers or board of directors mandates.

As discussed in section II(C), firms can take deliberate actions: instituting antitakeover charter amendments, chartering in states with antitakeover statutes, and granting golden parachutes that make removing managers difficult. Studies have also found other firm characteristics to discourage the removal of managers, such as firm size (the log of real 1980 dollar sales), R&D intensity (R&D divided by sales), the fraction of shares held by the top 4 owners, and Tobin's q.[29] Besides these variables, I also investigated a possible proxy for manager entrenchment—the manager turnover rate—using data collected from *Forbes* magazine between 1970 and 1989. Of course, low turnover might simply imply that long-serving managers are doing a good job, rather than entrenchment. The turnover rate is defined as the annualized average rate at which chief executive officers lose their positions during the sample period. The higher the managerial turnover rate, the less entrenched these officers are assumed to be, and thus the less credible is a firm's commitment to retain the manager when predation becomes necessary.

The theoretical discussion in section II, however, concentrates only on the costs of credible commitments and ignores the benefits from predation. While it is possible that the benefits from predation are the same across all industries, the return from making commitments may vary across industries because the same commitments may be more credible in some circumstances than in others. I reran the regressions with a new variable measuring the average rate at which firms in each SIC code are either accused or convicted of predation.[30]

Using these variables, table 2.8 displays three logit regressions predicting which firms in the COMPUSTAT data set faced predation charges.[31] The first two logits compare the characteristics of the firms charged with predation during their alleged predatory periods with all the firms in the COMPUSTAT data set never accused of predation as well as with the allegedly predatory firms during their nonpredatory years. The endogenous variable is a dummy variable that equals one whenever a firm is accused of predation during a particular year. Logits with and without the ownership concentration estimates and managerial turnover rates were reported, although observations for those two variables were unavailable for almost a quarter of the sample. The third logit compares whether a firm was ever accused of predation with that firm's sample averages of the exogenous variables over all the years for which the data were available. This tests whether firms accused or convicted of predation were more likely over this entire time period to have restrictions that are claimed to entrench management and thus help ensure credible commitments.

The results in table 2.8 fail to support the hypothesis that firms charged with predation were more likely to have either high R&D, antitakeover charter amendments, high q's, high ownership concentration, or low management turnover. The results from the first specification even suggests that antitakeover laws significantly lower the probability that firms will be accused of predation, and the effect is very large—firms in states with antitakeover laws have a 71 percent lower probability of being accused. The second specification, which

Table 2.8 Logit regressions predicting years accused of predation (from NBER Manufacturing Panel)

Exogenous variables	In predation years without ownership concentration rates		In predation years with ownership concentration rates		In all years (using period averages)	
	Coefficient	χ^2	Coefficient	χ^2	Coefficient	χ^2
Antitakeover charter amendment	-0.4896	1.638	-0.632	2.289	-0.3519	0.202
Antitakeover law dummy	-0.7052	4.3699*	-0.640	3.194*	-3.567	0.545
Management turnover rate	—	—	-2.918	0.882	—	—
Industry-adjusted Tobin's q	-0.2547	0.881	-0.049	0.029	-0.1516	0.126
R&D intensity	6.1325	0.9196	0.894	0.0179	-11.44	0.351
Log of sales	0.915	44.337*	0.715	16.66*	1.098	15.19*
Fraction of shares held by top 4 owners	—	—	-0.055	0.202	—	—
Average annual rate that predation charges are brought by industry	29.925	157.4*	22.209	143.06*	—	—
Average rate that predation charges are brought against an industry's firms	—	—	—	—	9.224	22.58*
Intercept	-12.785	113.27*	-10.257	43.225*	-8.163	43.20*
Nonpredation years	6312		3004			
Predation years	68		57			
Nonpredation firms					664	
Predation firms					19	
2*Log-likelihood	-386.85*		-317.33*		-78.004*	

*Means the value is statistically significant at least at the .10 level.

controls for the fraction of shares held by the largest four owners, produces similar results, and again the presence of antitakeover laws implies a lower probability of firms being charged with predation.[32] Interestingly, after cases heard before the Ninth Circuit Court of Appeals are omitted, the firms with high ownership concentrations are significantly less likely to have been accused of predation. This further suggests that the Ninth Circuit cases were more likely to involve firms that lacked the attributes expected of predators.

All three specifications indicate that firm size, as measured by total sales, is also higher in predatory firms. While this result is also consistent with the tough manager theory of predation, it is difficult to give much credence to predation theory on the basis of this result alone because larger firms are also more likely to be sued. Simply by affecting more parties in the economy, larger firms run greater hazards of being sued.

Table 2.9 reruns the regressions in table 2.8, but excludes the observations for predatory firms that were not convicted. If the firms that actually committed predation tend to be convicted more often than innocent firms, focusing only on convicted firms should be more likely to produce coefficients with the signs predicted by the tough manager predation theory. The endogenous variable is now a dummy variable that equals one whenever a firm is convicted of predation during a particular year. In keeping with the exclusion of firms accused but not convicted of predation, the first two specifications control for how the returns to predation vary across industries, using the average annual rate that an industry's firms are convicted of predation. Similarly, the third specification now uses the average rate that firms are convicted by industry. (The variable for concentration of share ownership was no longer included in the third specification since the specification did not converge.)

The results in table 2.9, like the ones in table 2.8, fail to support the hypothesis that firms charged with predation were more likely to have either high R&D, antitakeover charter amendments, high Tobin's q's, high ownership concentration, or low management turnover. The second specification provides some evidence consistent with the tough manager theory by showing that the fraction of shares held by the largest four owners is greatest for firms accused of predation. However, with firms accused of predation averaging ownership concentration rates of only .24, the coefficient on the fraction of ownership fails to be economically significant. The large negative and significant coefficient for R&D intensity in the second specification and

Table 2.9 Logit regressions predicting predation years for those cases where the firms were convicted (from NBER Manufacturing Panel)

Exogenous variables	In predation years for convicted firms without ownership		In predation years for convicted firms with ownership		In all years for convicted firms (using period averages)	
	Coefficient	χ^2	Coefficient	χ^2	Coefficient	χ^2
Antitakeover charter amendment	-1.1065	1.7994	-1.688	2.054	-2.8054	2.2269
Antitakeover law dummy	-0.2270	0.1737	0.6418	0.843	-1.4112	0.2971
Management turnover rate	—	—	-6.7951	0.437	—	—
Industry-adjusted Tobin's q	-0.7945	2.3298	-0.746	0.930	-0.8803	1.6477
R&D intensity	-18.259	0.6929	-89.590	3.2799*	-34.8405	1.0363
Log of sales	1.0351	15.131*	1.1145	2.2871	1.3085	8.9716*
Fraction of shares held by top 4 owners	—	—	0.0431	3.438*	—	—
Average annual rate that firms are convicted for predation by industry	38.473	89.151*	46.729	29.446*	—	—
Average rate that firms are convicted by industry	—	—	—	—	8.3316	15.26*
Intercept	-14.58	40.78*	-16.395	6.8849*	-9.4726	22.995
Nonpredation years	6344		3036			
Predation years	19		13			
Nonpredation firms					676	
Predation firms					7	
Log-likelihood	148.2*		74.68*		39.84*	

*Means the value is statistically significant at least at the .10 level.

the large negative coefficient for antitakeover amendments both contradict the tough manager theory. The firm size variable is again significant, but in only two of the three specifications.

As discussed in section III(C), the specifications shown in table 2.8 were reestimated, but the set of predation cases were limited to firms whose primary output involved items for which predation was said to have occurred. Only the coefficients on firm size are still consistent with the tough manager hypothesis and also statistically significant. I was unfortunately unable to rerun the regressions shown in table 2.9 with this smaller sample because none of these six firms were convicted of predation.

A potential problem with these logit regressions is that the coefficient estimates are not stable across specifications. To assess how serious this problem is, the range of coefficients and coefficient significance levels was found after running all possible subsets of the logits in table 2.8 using the global specification search method suggested by Leamer (1983). Panel A of table 2.10 shows the range of coefficients and their chi-squares for 256 regressions. The results are generally consistent with those reported in table 2.8. State antitakeover laws and firm size, as measured the log of sales, are significantly related to predation in all specifications. While the coefficients for antitakeover provisions, state antitakeover laws, and ownership concentration are usually the opposite of what the predation theory based upon managerial entrenchment suggests, the coefficients for managerial turnover, R&D intensity, and sales provide some support for the theory. The coefficients on antitakeover charter amendments are almost always negative, and it is significantly negative in 82 percent of the specifications. The estimated coefficients for ownership concentration reject the predation theory in that they are always negative, and in more than half of the specifications they are significantly so. By comparison, neither the significant negative coefficients for managerial turnover nor the significant positive coefficients for R&D intensity provide as consistent support for the reputational theory of predation, with neither variable being significant more than one-third of the time.

Panel B of table 2.10 tests the differences in means of these management entrenchment proxies across three sets of data: the years during which firms were charged with predation, the years when firms were not accused of predation, and years for which firms were convicted of predation. Comparing the mean characteristics for firms

Table 2.10 The Range of Possible Estimates

Panel A. Range of coefficients in all subset logit regressions

Endogenous variables	Minimum value	χ^2	Maximum value	χ^2
Antitakeover provision	−.871	4.03***	.097	0.06
State antitakeover law	−.711	3.74**	−.578	3.02*
Management turnover rate	−5.71	3.60*	0.85	0.18
Industry-adjusted Tobin's q	−.292	1.40	0.231	0.91
R&D intensity	0.18	0.01	9.70	3.92**
Log of sales	.60	10.0***	0.97	53.8***
Ownership concentration	−0.040	6.08**	−0.0028	0.06
Average annual rate that predation charges are brought by industry	26.2	138.5***	35.7	160.2***

NOTE: Range of coefficients and coefficient chi-squares in first two logit regressionsin table 2.6 using all possible subsets of the variables.
*Statistically significant at least at the .10 level.
**Statistically significant at least at the .05 level.
***Statisitically significant at least at the .01 level.

Panel B. Univariate comparisons

Variable	Mean nonpredation years (1)	Mean predation years (2)	Comparing (1) and (2) t-statistic (3)	Mean predation years for convicted firms (4)	Comparing (1) and (4) t-statistic (5)
Antitakeover charter amendment	22.2% (7953)	26.3% (68)	0.70	10.5% (19)	1.23
State antitakeover law	38.9% (6166)	29.4% (68)	1.47	42.1% (19)	0.28
Management turnover rate	11.0% (7953)	9.2% (57)	2.67***	8.6% (19)	3.788***
Industry-adjusted Tobin's q	0.0002% (6811)	−.026 (68)	0.34	0.059% (19)	7.38***
R&D intensity	0.8% (7953)	1.3% (68)	2.06**	1.3% (19)	1.00
Log of sales	6.31% (7953)	7.16% (68)	6.23***	7.43% (19)	2.88**
Ownership concentration	24.1% (3573)	21.0% (57)	1.06	22.9% (13)	0.14

NOTE: T-tests of differences in means of proxies for management entrenchment in predation and nonpredation years. Sample sizes shown in parentheses. Starred variables are statistically significant at the .05 level or better.
**Statistically significant at least at the .05 level.
***Statistically significant at least at the .01 level.

in the nonaccused and accused categories produces three significant differences: firms accused of predation were much more likely to have larger sales, be more R&D intensive, and have lower managerial turnover rates than were firms never charged with predation. The section that compares the firms that were convicted and cut prices with those that were never charged produces some evidence consistent with the tough manager theory. The means for sales, industry adjusted Tobin's q, and management turnover rates support the tough manager theory.

With the exception of the sales variable, the 262 regressions and the univariate results indicate: (1) the vast majority of characteristics thought to ensure management entrenchment are *not* associated with higher rates of accusations or convictions for predation and (2) even when significant results are obtained, they do not hold up consistently across specifications. On this last point, none of the variables that are significant in table 2.8, other than the log of sales, are significant and of the predicted sign in table 2.9, and the reverse is also true.[33]

E. Explaining Managerial Entrenchment

Finally, I sought to investigate further whether predatory firms were more likely to retain managers during alleged predation.[34] To do this, I regressed the annual managerial turnover (a variable that equals one if there was a turnover during a given year) on the dummy variables for PREDATION FIRM and CONVICTED AND PRICE DROP FIRM and/ or the dummy variables for PREDATION YEAR and CONVICTED AND PRICE DROP YEAR used earlier. I also controlled for: the manager's age and age squared; his years as CEO with the company and those years squared; measures of firm size, as given by the log of sales and employment; and the other variables used in tables 2.8, 2.9, and 2.10 which were related to managerial entrenchment.

Table 2.11 indicates that only a few of the variables normally associated with managerial entrenchment seem to help explain the rate at which CEOs leave office. Yet neither firms convicted or accused of predation nor firms during the years of alleged predation had higher turnover rates than did other firms. Thus, turnover might well be related to entrenchment, but entrenchment does not seem to explain predation. While five of the eight coefficients for dummy variables identifying predatory firms are negative, as the reputational theory of predation would suggest, none is statistically significant. Nor do the dummy variables identifying predatory firms become statistically

Table 2.11 Logit regressions predicting whether managers will leave during a particular year (from NBER Manufacturing Panel)

	Endogenous variable: Whether a firm's manager was removed during a particular year					
	Controlling for dummy variables identifying which firms were accused of predation		Controlling for dummy variables identifying which years during which predation occurred		Controlling for dummy variables identifying which firms were committing predation and the years during which predation is said to have occurred, plus industry dummy variables	
Exogenous variables	Coefficient	χ^2	Coefficient	χ^2	Coefficient	χ^2
Predation firm dummy	0.1101	0.1691	—	—	0.1924	0.3948
Convicted and price drop firm dummy	−0.4531	0.6749	—	—	−0.5930	0.8809
Predation year dummy	—	—	−0.3158	0.2549	−0.5668	0.6803
Convicted and price drop year dummy	—	—	−0.0743	0.0037	0.4303	0.0954
Antitakover charter amendment	−0.0061	0.0019	−0.0006	0.0000	−0.0761	0.2317
Antitakover law dummy	0.2317	3.0111*	0.2251	2.8478*	0.2441	3.1254*
Industry-adjusted Tobin's q	0.0945	0.4618	0.1074	0.6027	—	—
Tobin's q	—	—	—	—	0.1777	1.7467
R&D intensity	−7.6784	5.5001*	−7.4556	5.2098*	−8.4145	3.1805*
Age	−0.0453	0.1100	−0.0476	0.1215	−0.0413	0.0794

(continued)

Table 2.11 (continued)

Endogenous variable: Whether a firm's manager was removed in a particular year

Exogenous variables	Controlling for dummy variables identifying which firms were accused of predation		Controlling for dummy variables identifying years during which predation occurred		Controlling for dummy variables identifying which firms were commiting predation and the years during which predation is said to have occurred, plus industry dummy variables	
	Coefficient	χ^2	Coefficient	χ^2	Coefficient	χ^2
Age squared	−0.00055	0.1913	−0.00053	0.1787	−0.00068	0.2514
Years as CEO	−0.0340	4.3246*	−0.0336	4.2183*	−0.0422	6.0885*
Years as CEO squared	0.000558	2.9492*	0.00055	2.9058*	0.000644	3.6993*
Log of sales	0.00301	0.0002	0.00646	0.0010	−0.0552	0.0502
Log of employment	0.1964	2.5164	0.1894	2.3501	0.3117	2.1980
Fraction of shares held by top 4 owners	−0.00034	0.0072	−0.00067	0.0288*	−0.00069	0.0185
Intercept	2.2456	0.3606	2.2834	0.3734	2.5546	0.3809
Non-CEO removal years	2020		2020		2020	
CEO removal years	305		305		305	
Log-likelihood	1688.3*		1688.6*		1660.88*	

*Means the value is statistically significant at least at the .10 level.

significant when the dummy variables are included with only the measures of age, years as CEO, and firm size, or only the managerial entrenchment variables used in tables 2.8 through 2.10.[35] The only variables that were statistically significant at explaining managerial turnover are: R&D intensity, years as CEO, and the antitakeover law dummy. The coefficient on antitakeover laws is surprising since it implies that these laws actually increased managerial turnover. The coefficients for R&D intensity fit the traditional managerial entrenchment story and indicate that higher R&D intensity is related to less managerial turnover. The probability that managers will remain in office is closely linked to tenure. Managerial turnover also falls, though at a decreasing rate as tenure increases.

IV. Conclusion

This chapter finds no evidence that the assumptions underlying several models of predatory pricing are empirically tenable. In fact, the evidence appears to justify the courts' skepticism of game-theoretic models. The other evidence presented here, that firms supposedly engaged in predation raise managerial compensation when short-run profits rise, seems particularly difficult to reconcile with any notion of predation.

For tough managers' predatory commitments to be credible, the firm's contractual and noncontractual environment should make removing managers difficult. Simply hiring the correct type of manager is not sufficient if the manager can be removed whenever it actually becomes necessary to engage in predation. In addition, the incumbent manager should be rewarded for increasing output as opposed to increasing short-term profits. Yet, managers of the 28 firms alleged to have engaged in predation in the 1963–1982 period were not rewarded more for increasing output than were managers of other firms. If anything, the cases from the Ninth Circuit Court of Appeals imply that during those years that predation was allegedly taking place, increased output by the predator reduced the predator's managerial compensation. Little evidence supports the notion that managers of firms charged with predatory pricing were more entrenched than managers of other firms; for example, there is little difference in management turnover rates among predatory and nonpredatory firms. The results seriously challenge the relevance of game-theoretic predatory models by showing that their assumptions are inconsistent with actual firm behavior. Alternatively, the legal system may simply be unable to differentiate between innocent and guilty firms. Yet, this also brings the prosecution of predation cases into question. The evidence is consistent with the legal literature claiming that the decisions handed down by the Ninth Circuit Appeals Court are particularly suspect.

Not only do these results raise questions over courts' ability to identify predation even after the fact, but they provide even more reason to be dubious of claims that mergers should ever be prevented because of the possibility of future predation. This type of case can arise when competitors bring an antitrust suit claiming that a proposed merger of rivals will be anticompetitive. Competitors might claim that as a result of the merger, the merged firm will be more likely to engage in predatory activities that are designed to drive them out of business, and then raise prices to consumers. However, if courts are bad at identifying predation after the fact, it is very doubtful that they have a chance to identify it before the merger has even occurred.

Finally, this book joins the small literature on why managers of firms commit crimes. While other work has analyzed whether firms expecting lower future earnings are more likely to engage in fraud (Karpoff and Lott 1993 and Alexander and Cohen 1996), this chapter has investigated what characteristics alleged predatory firms exhibit. I found that alleged predators more often are large firms with managerial compensation schemes relying heavily on short-term profits. Firms accused of predation also tend to be located in states without antitakeover laws. Just as Bork (1978, 347–364) argues, the general picture is consistent with the laws being used to harass large profitable firms.

THREE

Nonprofit Objectives and Credible Commitments: What Does This Imply for Government Enterprises?

While a vast literature exists on predatory pricing by privately owned profit-maximizing firms, this literature has ignored public enterprises, which may turn out to act even more commonly as predators. In most nations, public enterprises compete against private firms in a wide variety of areas, including health care, postal services, education, transportation, and recreational services. Presumably private enterprises are perceived as the most obvious candidates to engage in predation because, unlike their public counterparts, they are profit maximizers. However, what is not recognized is that precisely because public enterprises are motivated by goals such as output maximization, rather than profit maximization, public enterprises face both higher returns to predation and higher returns to making credible the threats that are necessary for predation to succeed.[1]

Weather forecasting is one example where governments threatening below-cost prices may have prevented private forecasters from providing some services. Jeffrey Smith, executive director of the Association of Private Weather-Related Companies, has complained, "Many commercial meteorologists have been reluctant to take an increased role in forecasting because of the constant threat of government provision of these specialized forecasting services. Private firms do not know what service the government will choose to offer next for 'free'" (Ellig 1989b, A16). Hauser (1985, 23) discusses a case where a private meteorology service lost a paying customer (a television station) when the National Weather Service office started providing specialized forecasts free of charge. Hauser (p. 42) concludes, "Current federal ag-weather policy, either advertently or inadver-   *61* tently, has the effect of deterring investment by private meteorology in agricultural weather services."[2]

Another vastly more important case involves schooling. Take the case of higher education. Between 1965 and 1985, while public tuitions have declined from 22 to 18 percent of the level of private ones, the percentage of students enrolled in private institutions has fallen from 52 to 27 percent (U.S. Department of Commerce 1989). The idea of below-cost pricing sometimes also arises around public universities as private firms complain over unfair competition with state university-operated bookstores, food handling, and entertainment services (Hill 1990a, b). These complaints may arise in part because these operations often do not include building rent in determining prices and enjoy special tax-exemptions.

Interestingly, the U.S. government frequently accuses firms operated by other governments of predatory practices. For example, it accused China's space program of engaging in predation and forced that program to make changes in its pricing policies before American firms were allowed to purchase its services (Logsdon and Williamson 1989). This lends some credence to the view that even the U.S. government sees predation by public enterprises as a potential problem. While the United States may have been correct in charging China with predation, another possibility is that the Chinese were simply making a sunk investment through incurring a loss in the current period in order to produce a quality-guaranteeing reputation (e.g., see Darby and Lott 1989, 94–97). I will defer providing systematic evidence on these questions until the next chapter.

This chapter will first analyze the importance of output maximization in the context of predation and then show how the social costs of government bureaus are increased by the ability to price discriminate. Section II discusses the objective functions of private and public enterprises in terms of the existing literature on private predatory behavior as well as the applicability of the typical definition of predation to public enterprises. Arguments for why the returns to predation by public enterprises are higher than for private ones are examined in section III. Section IV shows why the threat of predation by public enterprises allows them to charge above competitive prices *without* encouraging new entry by private enterprises. Unlike private firms, public enterprises are more credible in making predatory commitments since they are made better off by the very act of predation and not just by the long-run returns from having eliminated competition. The final section demonstrates why public enterprises can predate even when their market share is small.

II. Predation by Private and Public Enterprises

Predation by a private firm hinges on the firm credibly committing itself to predation and communicating that fact to all potential competitors. Some have argued that such a predatory reputation arises from asymmetric information between established firms and potential entrants with regard to the predatory firm's objective function (Milgrom and Roberts 1982b, 285).[3] Potential entrants are misled into believing that there is some probability that the established firm is not a profit maximizer (e.g., that it values eliminating competitors) so that the potential entrant takes the threats of reduced prices seriously and declines entry. The established competitor is thus left alone so it can maximize its monopoly profits. Yet, given that the only reason established firms are predatory is to increase profits, it is hard to believe that all potential entrants systematically make the mistake of assuming that established firms operate according to some behavioral rule other than strict profit maximization. If predatory firms do not have the ability to convince potential future entrants that their entry will initiate further predation, predation will prove costly without generating much (if any) benefit. The belief that firms are profit maximizers is so widely held that it is difficult to accept the assumption that all potential competitors believe otherwise.

In contrast to private firms, government agencies are typically viewed as adhering to some other objective function, such as maximizing the bureau's size or output (e.g., Niskanen 1971, and 1975, and Lindsay 1976).[4] Several reasons why public enterprises would maximize output have been advanced. First, since incentive compensation schemes based on managers receiving a share of the profits are not allowed and monitoring is costly, public enterprises may maximize output or discretionary budgets because these strategies could yield benefits to their managers.[5] A larger output can raise salaries, open greater opportunities for consulting or contracting with the agency after retirement, increase utility if the bureaucrat intrinsically values the mission of the agency, and increase the prestige that comes from being associated with a larger agency (Niskanen 1971, 38, and Johnson and Libecap 1989b, 448).[6] While the maximizing of output should presumably be just as visible to the politicians who monitor agency behavior as it is to the economists who study these questions, the empirical evidence suggests that such behavior persists (Niskanen 1975; Lindsay 1976).[7]

Alternative arguments, which do not involve systematic mistakes by politicians, may include a desire on the part of politicians to create wealth transfers, either to consumers by charging low prices for the products sold by these public enterprises or to their public employees through methods that are relatively hard for voters to monitor. The particular reason that public enterprises value output maximization is not important. The crucial assumption here is simply that public enterprises value increased output more than private enterprises do.

While the Niskanen-type losses directly borne by the output-maximizing public enterprise are well understood, a previously unrecognized second type of loss also exists. In order to sell their excess production, public firms have to price their output below the market price and thereby cause more efficient firms to be eliminated. Technically this fits the definition of predation used in industrial organization. For example, Isaac and Smith (1985, 330) describe the two characteristics of predatory pricing in the literature as: (1) "the price charged by the predator is lower than would be optimal in a simple myopic (short-run) pricing strategy" and (2) "the price has the effect of preventing entry, or driving out and preventing reentry, of the prey." There is nothing in this definition to distinguish between predation by the government and private organizations. Even if their reduction in price is based on differing motivations, a price cut to obtain new customers imposes the same costs on rivals. It does not matter whether it is done because public managers value a larger agency or because private managers want to eliminate competition.[8]

Yet, predation by a private firm involves more than simply driving existing firms out of business. When a private firm later obtains the benefits from successful predation by charging monopoly prices, it risks making entry attractive again for potential competitors. While public output-maximizing firms are unlikely to take these benefits through charging a single monopoly price (since the continued use of the initial predatory price would result in a larger output), eliminating competition allows output-maximizing public enterprises to use above-competitive prices obtained from one group of customers to subsidize below-cost pricing to another group. For example, the public enterprise could price discriminate and use the resulting above-competitive profits on the inframarginal units to subsidize its losses on the marginal units, thus further expanding its output. As when private firms raise prices, these supracompetitive prices produce incentives for new entry. However, public enterprises have an advantage in credibly committing to lower prices again when their market share is challenged, since they are perceived as having a nonprofit-maximizing objective, and entry reduces output by eliminating their ability to engage in cross-subsidization. Predation not only increases output in the short run but can allow even greater increases after the entrant is driven from the market.

III. Predation and the Government Bureau's Objective Function

While profit maximization seems to adequately characterize the motivation of private firms, I have discussed why other objectives might better describe a public sector firm. For example, suppose in line with Niskanen (1975, 621) that an agency maximizes its discretionary budget (the difference between its budget and the cost of producing the output). This is essentially profit maximization. Assume the appropriate cost and demand curves are as shown in figure 3.1, where the subscript P indicates the cost curves for the predator and the subscript V those of the victim. If firm P acts as a competitive profit maximizer, it charges a price of $2.50 and sells 44 units. The market price would be determined by the market demand curve intersecting the sum of the two marginal cost curves, at 52 units. Likewise, firm V would sell 8 units. The resulting profits would presumably be spent on perquisites for the bureau's employees.

Niskanen's analysis states that, at the other extreme, bureaucrats may value only the size of their agency's output and not the size of their discretionary budgets (1975, 621). This view suggests that bureaucrats' salaries vary on the basis of the number of individuals for which they have responsibility. An individual bureaucrat's chances for advancement are thus related to the size of his agency. For simplicity, I initially assume, unlike Niskanen, that this firm cannot engage in price discrimination. Suppose firm P maximizes its long-run output subject to a non-negative profit constraint by setting price so that the firm's average cost curve intersects the market demand curve. It will set price equal to $2.20 with a corresponding output of 60, which increases its sales from $110 to $132. The output for firm V, assuming no sunk costs, is reduced to zero. Firm P earns zero economic profits and can maintain that price since no takeover mechanisms exist for public enterprises.[9]

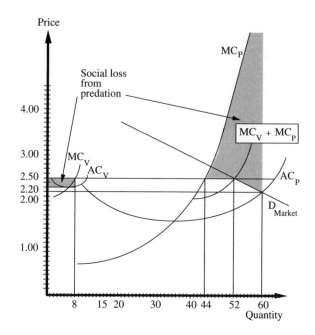

Figure 3.1 The social cost of predation by large public enterprises in the absence of price discrimination

The social loss from this predation is equal to the sum of the shaded areas shown in figure 3.1 and consists of two parts: the social costs from excessive production and the higher production costs due to predation. Predation creates additional production costs equal to the difference between the predatory firm's cost of producing the output between 44 and 52 units and the cost of the victim firm's producing its first 8 units. This difference equals the shaded triangular area between outputs of 44 and 52 below firm P's marginal cost curve plus the rectangular shaded area above firm V's total cost of producing 8 units. (In the absence of the victim firm having any fixed costs, this increase in production costs equals the entire area between the industry marginal cost curve ($MC_v + MC_p$) and the public producer's marginal cost curve (MC_p) up to 52 units.) This cost of predation through higher production costs is borne even if industry output remains unchanged at 52 units. The Niskanen-type costs from excess production are represented by the sail-shaped area between the market demand curve and the public provider's marginal cost curve over the range between 52 to 60 units of output.[10] Interestingly, predation makes the Niskanen-type costs significantly more severe than recognized in the previous analyses.

Public firms may also enjoy some additional advantages to predation not obtained by private enterprises. Niskanen (1975, 637) has argued that where private alternatives exist, the costs of legislators monitoring the agency are reduced, thus decreasing the level of rents that can be extracted by the agency. If Niskanen is correct, my discussion implies that successful predation eliminates such competition and thus makes monitoring more costly.[11] Public firms may benefit more from the absence of such a yardstick than private companies whose performance is constantly being evaluated through such mechanisms as the stock market.

A second advantage for public predators may be a greater ability to commit to predation than their private counterparts. This follows from the managers of public enterprises actually obtaining benefits from selling the product at the predatory price. Public firms would need only to convince potential competitors that they will do something that these competitors believe is in the public firm's managers' interest to do in the first place. Predatory private firms on the other hand face the more difficult task of convincing potential rivals that the predator is willing to forgo substantial profits in order to stop any new entry—something which is *not* in the predator's interest to do when it actually would have to be undertaken.

Some politicians who oversee these agencies may also value this predation to the extent that it subsidizes certain favored constituencies. For example, this may explain why many agencies such as the Federal Reserve, U.S. Forest Service, and Bureau of Land Management are not allowed to retain profits (or revenue) from sales and must turn them over to the U.S. Treasury. Shaw and Stroup (1989, 5) note that when the general Treasury rules were changed in 1987 so that the National Park Service could keep a small portion of the fees that it charged for park visits, the Park Service increased its rates from the average per person charge of $.21 and per car charge of $.39 in 1986 to $1.05 and $1.74 in 1987 (National Park Service 1989).[12] Since the Federal Reserve cannot retain the revenue from setting higher prices for check-clearing services, the Federal Reserve has an incentive to set the price well below its costs and take the benefits in the form of an increased quantity of its services demanded. Other explanations for below-cost pricing that do not rest upon shirking are also possible. For example, Lott (1990) argues that the below-cost pricing of public schooling combined with the use of geographically assigning students to public schools may have resulted from a desire to instill values not directly held by the students or their parents.

Finally, by eliminating private competitors, public enterprises may reduce the political opposition to their receiving increased subsidies. Public enterprises presumably value these subsidies if they allow for lower prices and expanded output. The organized political opposition to legally imposed entry barriers for private enterprises may also be reduced. The elimination of public competitors may be especially valued if there is free-riding in lobbying for subsidies (Lott 1987b).

IV. Price Discrimination and Its Effect on the Social Cost of Predation

The preceding section describes a static result: low prices and the elimination of competitors are both consequences of output maximization by public enterprises. Yet predation is usually viewed as a more dynamic process with prices changing after competitors have been eliminated. There are several reasons to believe that public and private enterprises will obtain the long-run benefits from predation differently. While predatory private firms charge monopoly prices after driving potential competitors from the market, output-maximizing public enterprises would prefer to keep on setting price equal to average cost rather than adopting a single monopoly price. Even if the public enterprise's managers were tempted to maximize their discretionary budgets, federal agencies must turn over a large portion of their revenue from sales as well as any operating profits to the Treasury. Agencies also face the constraint that Congress judges them by the amount of output that they produce for a given level of expenditures (Lindsay 1976, 1065). Government bureaus may thus find that setting a monopoly price either results in the Treasury's taking the additional profits or causes pressure from Congress if the agency spends its monopoly profits on perks. Given these constraints, managers are likely to prefer extracting benefits through increasing agency size.[13] In fact, as noted earlier, Congress may even have set up the constraints in order to maximize output.

Yet, some public enterprises actually face an alternative either to setting a simple monopoly price or to setting price equal to average cost: if price discrimination against the inframarginal customers is possible, supracompetitive profits on those units can be used to subsidize below-cost sales at the margin.[14] Examples of government agencies using the rents from some output to subsidize other production and thus avoiding restrictions on having to turn revenue over to the Treasury can be seen in the U.S. Forest Service's management of the timber industry (see Johnson 1985, and Muraoka and Watson 1985) and the Bureau of Land Management's administration of the livestock grazing fees (Libecap 1981). For example, the U.S. Forest Service often requires that logging companies bid on both timber that is profitable to cut and timber that is not. Logging companies then bear the loss from cutting the unprofitable timber in exchange for the right to cut the desirable timber, but these tie-in sales increase the total amount of wood harvested and reduce the overall payments from the private firms to the government agency. Cross-subsidization also arises between timber and recreational uses of the land and between areas of high-value and low-value timber when the profits in the one area are used to pay for road building and timber stand improvement (see Johnson 1985, 129–131). While the discussion here will assume that price discrimination takes the form of charging different prices for the same good, a possibly more prevalent form of price discrimination by public enterprises, which does not alter the analysis, is to charge the same price while varying the quality of a good.[15]

One widely recognized instance of charging different prices based upon the elasticity of demand is the Postal Service's practice of charging a monopoly price for first class mail and then using the proceeds to subsidize the provision of overnight mail delivery, which it suffers losses on. The 1988 increase in first class postal rates to 25 cents coincided with a simultaneous reduction in the U.S. Postal Service domestic overnight express mail charges to $8.75, despite the fact that the express mail service was already losing money at the higher price. (For evidence of the use of this type of cross-subsidization in the past, see U.S. Postal Service 1973, 6.) Six private air-express companies have also sued the Postal Service over the government agency's reduction in overseas express mail from $18 to $8.75 (Ruffenach 1989, 4). The private firms argued that "the low rate takes advantage of the monopoly that the Postal Service has in other classes of mail—a monopoly, the plaintiffs say, that allows it to subsidize international express delivery." The U.S. Postal Service reported that the rate reductions were responsible for a 66 percent (or 96,336 package) increase in the number of packages shipped over the same month the previous year.

To return to the modeling: Price discrimination allows firm P to increase its output beyond where the market demand curve equals the firm's average cost and still earn a zero profit. If firm P desires to maximize output, it can now attain an even larger output, but the social loss will also increase by the additional area between the industry's demand curve and the predator's marginal cost curve. A government bureau's ability to price discriminate is potentially much more socially costly than a private firm's. Price discrimination by private firms can be socially beneficial to the extent it moves output closer to that obtained under perfectly competitive markets. In the extreme case of perfect price discrimination, the output of a profit-maximizing monopolist is the same as that of a perfectly competitive firm. This would also hold if a public firm were to maximize its discretionary budget. However, a Niskanen-type output maximizer lowers society's wealth to the extent that it engages in any price discrimination, since any additional revenue will be used to increase an already too high level of output.[16]

Price discrimination, however, produces the threat of potential entry. While entry for a profit-maximizing predator results in either no change in total output (the case of perfect price discrimination) or an increase in output, a price-discriminating, output-maximizing firm would actually lower output by more than the increased output from new entrants. Entry reduces the public enterprise's output both through the lower prices offered to some of the public firm's customers and also through reducing its profits (thus reducing its ability to subsidize below-cost sales). At the very least, if entry resulted in the output-maximizing public enterprise's lowering output to below the 60 units shown in figure 3.1, *its interests would be best served by either no longer price discriminating and instead charging all customers $2.20 or price discriminating only at prices below which the new entrants would find it unprofitable to operate.* Any new entrants would then leave the industry, as discussed in section III. In order to discourage entry which would normally arise from discriminatory pricing, the public firm needs only to commit to an action that is in its interest should entry occur. The predatory public firm has an advantage over profit-maximizing firms in discouraging any entry that results from its price discrimination. While predation by a profit-maximizing firm requires that it temporarily forgo profits, predation by an output-maximizing firm may be necessary to maintain a higher output. An analogous assumption to a private firm's forgoing profits is for a public firm to reduce prices to $2.20 *before* entry drives its output below 60 units.

Private firms also face an additional constraint in deterring entry which is not borne by public enterprises: the antitrust merger guidelines. Because of a private predator's already large market shares, the guidelines will likely prevent the selling of the victim's assets to private predators, restrictions that do not apply to the government. This provides a difficulty for private predation in areas where capital facilities are specialized, long-lived, and transferable. Here other new entrants would be able to purchase the assets of the victim at prices that discount the observed, credible predatory behavior of the incumbent firm. Consequently, the predator cannot easily eliminate competition: driving out the first entrant would simply result in a new competitor with lower costs than the first entrant. If the public predator is able to buy up the victim's assets, it can forestall the entrance of a new competitor. For public enterprises, this activity may take the form of the government acquiring formerly private universities (e.g., George Mason University School of Law, University of Buffalo, University of Houston, and University of Pittsburgh) after driving the initial owners into bankruptcy.[17]

Throughout my analysis of government enterprises I have not had to rely on the traditional assumptions associated with successful predation by private enterprises, such as the predator's having sufficient staying power, the existence of entry or reentry barriers for competitors, or the period of predation not being too long.

V. Predation by "Tiny" Public Enterprises

If predation is to occur at all, theory predicts that it will be done only by profit-maximizing firms with an overwhelming share of the market and those that have substantial cost advantages (e.g., Bork 1978, 150–153). Yet, as can be seen from figure 3.2, this is not necessary for public enterprises. It may still pay for a public enterprise that possesses neither size nor cost advantages to engage in predation. In this case, the predatory public enterprise has both a higher minimum point for its average cost curve and a relatively small output. Predation consists of setting average cost equal to price. In equilibrium, the predatory public enterprise increases its output from 8 to 11 units while the private profit-maximizing victim reduces its output from 44 to 43 units. Overall industry output then rises to 54 units, with a price of

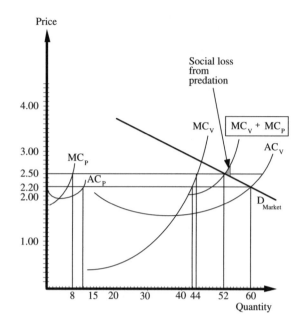

Figure 3.2   The social cost of predation by small public enterprises assuming no price discrimination

$2.30. The social cost of this public predation is shown by the shaded area between the industry's marginal cost curve and the demand curve over the range of the excess production. As long as this tiny predator is able to cover its average costs, it continues to be predatory unless some other new constraint is imposed on its behavior. As noted earlier, it is possible that the short-run loss to public predation is even larger. The main difference from my earlier discussion is that there is little danger of the predator's driving the large, efficient private victim out of business. However, if there existed other small private firms with higher minimum average costs, they might be driven out of business.

VI. Conclusion

Many economists believe that predation is least likely when firms are thought by their competitors to be profit maximizers. Yet, while public corporations have been accused of maximizing various objectives, profits does not usually head the list. To the extent that public enterprises value maximizing output rather than profits, as empirical evidence discussed by Lindsay (1976) and Niskanen (1975) indicates, the social costs of public ownership may be substantially greater than previously believed. Predatory commitments by public enterprises are more credible since, unlike private firms, they have been shown to be made better off by the very act of predation and not just by the long-run returns from having eliminated competition. Whether public enterprises value output maximization because of either shirking or a desire to create transfers is not important to the arguments presented here; the crucial assumption is simply that public enterprises value output maximization relative to private enterprises. While predation is only likely (if ever) to occur for large, relatively low-cost, profit-maximizing private firms, any size public enterprise can be predatory. In addition, if credible commitments by public enterprises are not viewed as particularly likely, it should be even more doubtful that private enterprises can successfully make credible commitments.

FOUR

Are Government or Private Enterprises More Likely to Engage in Predatory Behavior?: Some International Evidence

As just noted in the last chapter, many economists believe that government-owned enterprises are motivated by goals such as output, employment, or revenue maximization (e.g., Niskanen 1971, 1974, and 1975, and Lindsay 1976). Building on this work, I argued that if government enterprises are motivated by these nonprofit-maximizing objectives, attainment of these goals will be facilitated by the firm's pricing below cost and, by its actions, causing the eventual exit of its competitors. While both government and privately owned firms benefit from the long-term reduction in competition resulting from a successful strategy of below-cost pricing, only the government-owned enterprise also benefits from the short-term increase in its output required to undertake this strategy and from never again having to lower price and increase output in response to future entry.

For each of these reasons, a direct implication of government and private enterprises' differing objective functions is that public firms will be more likely to engage in below-cost pricing.[1] This chapter seeks to test the hypothesis by comparing the relative frequencies with which charges of below-cost pricing are brought against private and government enterprises. In the domestic market, such charges would most naturally be brought under the antitrust laws as predatory pricing. A couple of considerations, however, hinder testing the hypothesis that government enterprises are more likely to engage in "predatory-like" behavior. First, in some countries including the United States, government-owned enterprises are explicitly exempted from most antitrust scrutiny (Wiley 1986). Second, govern-

74

ments are unlikely to bring charges against the very corporations they own. For both of these reasons, the hypothesis is tested using data from charges of below-cost pricing brought by governments against firms in other countries. Such disputes are brought under a country's anti-dumping laws, which provide legal remedies against foreign firms exporting at prices "below normal value" and which "materially injure" the competing industry in the importing country.[2] Particular attention will be focused here upon the comparative pricing behavior of exporting firms in market and nonmarket economies, where the divergence between private and government ownership of enterprises is most acute.

Dumping charges involving exporters based in nonmarket countries have received substantial attention. In one such dispute, the United States accused the Chinese government of pricing below cost in the satellite launch services market (Foley 1988, 29).[3] In another widely publicized case, the United States accused Poland of selling motorized golf carts for less than its cost of production (Ehrenhaft 1989, 303). More typically, trade disputes with nonmarket economies have involved less exotic products where quality is a lesser concern. Products involved in past dumping disputes include candles, cotton towels, wooden clothespins, natural bristle paint brushes, barbed wire, carbon steel wire and sheets, potassium chloride, and steel wire nails (United States International Trade Commission 1984, 227–231). Government-owned firms operating in market economies also have been accused of unfair trading practices. In 1987, for example, the United States filed a formal request with the GATT to investigate charges that the Airbus consortium had sold wide-body commercial aircraft at prices "below true manufacturing costs" for an extended period of time (Mecham 1987, 35, 39).[4]

The data used here require addressing the concern that international political motives may bias dumping investigations. In particular, exporting firms in nonmarket economies may be subject to a disproportionate number of dumping complaints for political reasons unrelated to their actual export-pricing behavior.[5] This is important given the difficulties involved in measuring the costs of firms in nonmarket economies and the possibilities that systematic political biases might exist in interpreting and enforcing the rules. A major focus of this chapter, therefore, is to remove any influence of such political biases upon the central economic hypothesis being tested. Two potential sources of bias are identified and tested for. First, using cross-country data on anti-dumping investigations conducted by governments in different regional and military alliances, the chapter tests for the presence of defense-related political biases and explicitly controls for them. The number of dumping complaints that would still have been brought against nonmarket firms in the absence of political biases is compared with the number of cases actually brought against state-owned firms. Second, the distribution of anti-dumping protection accusations across industries in market economies may be correlated with the distribution of their imports from nonmarket economies. A test for this potential bias is to see if nonmarket countries' exports are relatively concentrated in the more heavily protected sectors.

Obviously, governments may not be very good at determining whether firms are charging below cost and, just as many are skeptical of the government's ability to enforce antitrust laws properly, it is possible that few if any of the findings of guilt actually involve cases of below-cost pricing.[6] However, to the extent that people believe that governments bring cases that are at least weakly related to true below-cost pricing cases, the theory of greater predation by government enterprises predicts that we should find higher rates at which cases are brought against government and private enterprises. The question analyzed here is whether governments act as if they believe that other governments' enterprises pose a greater predatory threat than private firms from other countries.

II. The Behavior of Government-Owned Enterprises in Nonmarket Economies

If the common presumption is correct that government enterprises are more likely than private firms to pursue objectives such as maximizing the agency's size or output, my earlier discussion in chapter 3 implies that government enterprises should be more likely to engage in predation. In the case of nonmarket economies, additional nonprofit-maximizing objectives are likely to characterize firms' behavior.[7] Many of these objectives may be set directly by the politicians that oversee the government-owned firms. For example, government enterprises are typically encouraged to fulfill production targets and increase employment, both of which are consistent with output- maximizing behavior (Wolf 1988, 11–13, and Holzman 1966, 240–241). Export markets provide one outlet for the increased production that both of these objectives promote. Nonmarket countries also may use government enterprises to maximize export revenues in order to obtain foreign currency (Wolf 1988, 12). If firm demand is elastic because competition exists, reducing its output below the point where price equals marginal cost will reduce export revenues. By contrast, expanding output beyond the point where price equals average cost is consistent with maximization of foreign currency receipts. The particular reason behind government enterprises valuing output maximization, however, is not important to the arguments presented here. The crucial assumption is that government enterprises value output maximization more than private enterprises do.

Elimination of foreign competitors, as required by predation, also assists state enterprises in acquiring additional foreign currency revenues. These additional revenues may come from the firm's subsequent ability to reduce sales and charge the monopoly price or from the facilitation of price discrimination. In the case of perfect price discrimination, maximizing output and maximizing foreign currency revenues are identical. As with predation by private enterprises, however, charging higher prices after the elimination of competitors attracts new rivals to the market.[8] Yet, unlike private profit-maximizing firms, which find predation very costly, foreign currency-maximizing government enterprises are actually made better off by lowering price (increasing output) in response to new entry.[9] Entry also makes the firm's perceived demand curve more elastic, further increasing the benefit the revenue-maximizing state enterprise receives from lowering price and increasing output.

For these reasons, I expect that, relative to profit-maximizing enterprises, government enterprises will be able to make more credible commitments to lower prices in response to new entry. As explained in chapter 3, government enterprises also face higher returns from below-cost pricing since they benefit not only from the long-term reduction in competition, but also from the short-term increase in their output required to undertake the below-cost pricing strategy. These greater returns should be manifested in a higher frequency of below-cost selling among public firms than among their privately owned counterparts.

Although testing whether government enterprises are more likely than private enterprises to engage in below-cost pricing is the ultimate objective, it is not feasible to do so in the context of a single economy. As mentioned earlier, government enterprises are usually exempt from their own antitrust laws and are unlikely to bring charges against the very corporations they own. For these reasons, the empirical work will focus on international anti-dumping suits. Both the old General Agreement on Tariffs and Trade (GATT) and the new World Trade Organization rules established a framework under which importing countries may investigate alleged dumping by foreign producers. Dumping involves a firm selling a product for "less than its normal value" and thereby "causing or threatening material injury to an established industry" in the importing country (GATT, Art. VI, Sec. 1). While calculations of whether a product is being sold below cost are made either by attempting to sum up all the costs in the production process or (when dealing with firms in nonmarket countries) by looking at related firms in market countries where input prices are more readily available, price discrimination can also serve as a substitute form of evidence (see Appendix 5a for a more detailed discussion of what constitutes dumping and the problems with these different definitions). Predation is also defined by two similar conditions: (1) that "the price charged by the predator [be] lower than would be optimal in a simple myopic (short-run) pricing strategy," and (2) that this "price [has] the effect of preventing entry, or driving out and preventing re-entry of the prey" (Isaac and Smith 1985, 330).[10]

In the United States, dumping complaints are filed with the International Trade Commission and the U.S. Department of Commerce. Appeals by private parties can be made to the Court of International Justice; if both parties operate in countries under the North American Free Trade Agreement, a special tribunal hears those cases. Governments may appeal decisions to the World Trade Organization.

The enforcement of anti-dumping laws is at least publicly motivated by the same concerns as predation in the industrial organization literature, and the below-cost definition of dumping under international trade law closely accords with the concept of predation. Nonmarket economies provide an easily identifiable set of government enterprises to study. It would have been interesting to include government agencies within market economies, but unfortunately a number of alternative measures are not available (e.g., measures of the percentage of a country's exports produced by state-owned firms, the percentage of different types of exports produced by government enterprises, and data on the number of individual cases brought against private or government enterprises). Some limited information is available on the percentage of the United States's dumping cases against market economies that focus on state enterprises, but this evidence will be left until section III(D). The question I will ask in the next section is whether dumping complaints and affirmative actions have been brought at a disproportionate rate against firms from nonmarket economies relative to their counterparts from market economies. While some economists who study nonmarket economies have pointed out that companies from those countries appear to dump more frequently, no systematic evidence has previously been provided.[11]

III. Empirical Methodology and Test Results

The sample of government enterprises consists of firms in nonmarket economies during the period 1980–1987. The data rely on the export pricing behavior of firms in a total of 59 countries, ten of which are nonmarket economies: Bulgaria, China, (former) Czechoslovakia, the (former) German Democratic Republic, Hungary, North Korea, Poland, Romania, the (former) Soviet Union, and (former) Yugoslavia.[12] Three sets of regressions were used to test the hypothesis that government enterprises are more likely to have dumping complaints filed against them. The first and second regression specifications, presented in section III(A), measure the rate at which dumping charges are brought and won against firms in market and nonmarket economies.[13] In these regressions, the number of initiated or affirmed anti-dumping investigations against foreign exporters is expressed as a function of the two countries' volume of trade, the exporting country's level of economic development, and the form of its market organization. The third set of regressions, presented in section III(B), control for the possibility that anti-dumping complaints are motivated by defense-related political goals. Section III(C) tests to see if a bias exists to the extent that nonmarket economies tend to export goods that are more politically protected from competition by market economies. Finally, section III(D) discusses two other possible biases.

A. The Rate of Dumping by Firms from Market and Nonmarket Economies

The cross-country data set of anti-dumping investigations was compiled from tabulations in Finger and Olechowski (1987) and United

Nations Conference on Trade and Development (1985–1989). The data include 59 countries whose exporters were subjected to anti-dumping actions by the United States, the EEC, Canada, Australia, and Finland over the period 1980–1987.[14] Together, these complaints accounted for 93 percent of all anti-dumping investigations initiated during this period (Jackson 1989a, 15). The pattern of dumping complaints against market and nonmarket economies by each of these jurisdictions is summarized in table 4.1.[15] While these initial data only allow us to indicate the type of economy against which the complaints were brought and not the exact identity of the country, the data indicate significant cross-country variation in the rate at which anti-dumping investigations were initiated and won. Section III(D) discusses how anti-dumping complaints are initiated and adjudicated. It also shows how this process seriously biases the following tests against us finding that government enterprises in nonmarket economies engage in below-cost pricing more frequently then firms in marker economies.[16]

I attempted to explain the number of complaints using the following cross-sectional regression:[17]

Table 4.1 The distribution of anti-dumping cases by countries bringing the complaints

	Initiated anti-dumping cases (1980–1987)							
	Austria	Australia	Canada	EEC	Finland	Spain	Sweden	USA	Total
Nonmarket	0	26	20	141	9	0	3	35	234
Market	1	436	250	321	13	1	4	381	1407
Total	1	462	270	462	22	1	7	416	1641

	Affirmative anti-dumping cases (1980–1986)						
	Austria	Australia	Canada	EEC	Spain	Sweden	USA	Total
Nonmarket	0	13	18	108	0	2	19	160
Market	2	219	140	213	0	0	195	769
Total	2	232	158	321	0	2	214	929

SOURCES: Finger and Olechowski 1987, table A8.4, and United Nations Conference on Trade and Development (1984–1989, Section 5).

NOTE: Unlike the data for Australia, Canada, EEC, Finland, and USA, the data for Austria, Spain, and Sweden do not identify the individual countries that the complaints are brought against. Data for Finland are not available for the affirmative dumping cases.

$$INITIATED_{i,j} = a_0 + a_1\ IMPORTS_{i,j} + a_2\ EXPORTS_{i,j}$$
$$+\ a_3\ REAL\ PERSONAL\ GDP_j \qquad (1)$$
$$+\ a_4\ NONMARKET_j + u_{i,j}$$

where $INITIATED_{i,j}$ = number of investigations by country i against
country j's exporters,

$IMPORTS_{i,j}$ = country i's total imports from country j,

$EXPORTS_{i,j}$ = country i's total exports to country j,

$REAL\ PERSONAL\ GDP_j$ = real per capita GDP in country j, and

$NONMARKET_j$ = a dummy that equals one for nonmarket
economies.

In addition to pooling the data across countries to estimate the average relationship between the number of anti-dumping investigations
and market organization, this chapter also reports separate results
for each of the five jurisdictions bringing the dumping complaints.

Data on bilateral trade flows were taken from the International
Monetary Fund's *Direction of Trade Yearbook* (1987a and 1989).[18]
The total value of imports from each trading partner is the most natural variable to convert the number of anti-dumping complaints into
a rate-of-investigation variable that can easily be compared across
countries. The number of anti-dumping disputes is expected to increase as the value of goods subject to investigation rises.

The cost to the "injured" country of imposing sanctions should be
directly related to the value of its exports to the country whose firm
is accused of dumping. Previous empirical studies of administered
protection in the United States, such as Takacs (1981), Magee and
Young (1987), and Salvatore (1989), have found a negative relationship between a country's bilateral trade balance and the number of
anti-dumping investigations or other import relief actions that they
initiate. One possible explanation for this finding is that, after holding
imports constant, countries that have larger exports to a trading partner potentially have more to lose as a result of retaliation to any
trade sanctions. The greater the cost of imposing sanctions, the fewer
sanctions that are expected to be imposed. Presumably, this reasoning is also applicable to imports, although it is impossible for the
number of dumping cases always to decline with higher imports since
the number of dumping cases is zero when imports are zero. Because
the relationship between anti-dumping complaints and exports (or
imports) need not be linear, alternative regression specifications that
included quadratic terms for these two variables were also estimated.

The real per capita GDP variable controlled for the level of economic development in the exporting country. These data were taken from the Penn World Table (Mark 4) reported in Summers and Heston (1988).[19] Finger, Hall, and Nelson (1982) have argued that governments perceive less developed countries as lacking the requisite resources or skills to exert political pressure on their own behalf in anti-dumping investigations. If this argument is true, governments may be more apt to pursue anti-dumping complaints against firms in countries with lower per capita income.[20] Alternatively, less developed countries are frequently given preferential treatment through lower tariffs designed to assist their economic development.[21] If developed countries also assist these less developed countries by enforcing anti-dumping provisions less rigorously, countries with lower per capita incomes may face fewer dumping complaints.

The final independent variable in regression (1) is a dummy that equals one for nonmarket economies and zero otherwise. The central hypothesis that government enterprises have a greater return to below-cost pricing predicts that the coefficient on the NONMARKET variable should be positive. I had hoped to find a quantitative measure of the percent of exports from each country in the sample arising from state-owned firms, but could not. This regrettably forced the use of a dummy variable for nonmarket economies. It is clear that this dummy variable imperfectly measures the extent of government ownership of exporting enterprises across countries. Obviously, while all firms in nonmarket economies are state-owned, there are many government enterprises that operate in market economies.[22] As section III(D) will show, using the NONMARKET dummy variable therefore yields a downward-biased estimate of the impact of market organization on dumping complaints. The more general issue of measurement error is discussed later.

The results for the initiated cases are reported in tables 4.2 and 4.3. Columns 1 and 2 of table 4.2 report the results for the different specifications pooling the data for countries that brought dumping charges. Table 4.3 breaks down the data by the five government entities bringing dumping charges. As measured by the adjusted R2 values, a significant portion of the cross-country variation in anti-dumping complaints is explained by the market organization, trade flow, and economic development variables. The one consistent finding across all of the regressions is that dumping cases are brought at higher rates against nonmarket economies than they are against mar-

Table 4.2 Explaining the number of initiated and affirmed anti-dumping cases (absolute t-statistics in parentheses)

Exogenous variables	Initiated cases (1980–1987)		Affirmed cases (1980–1986)	
	(1)	(2)	(3)	(4)
Nonmarket dummy	20.28868 (3.7105)	20.91968 (5.3007)	12.27042 (4.182)	12.539420 (4.4910)
Imports USA	0.000712 (2.0516)	−0.001169 (1.9521)	0.000241 (1.5862)	−0.000260 (0.7139)
Imports USA squared	—	0.2583 E−7 (2.8681)	—	0.6179 E−8 (1.0888)
Imports EEC	−0.9974 E−4 (0.6629)	−0.000424 (2.0368)	0.1043 E−4 (0.1689)	0.2533 E−4 (0.2369)
Imports EEC squared	—	0.1108E−9 (0.2605)	—	−0.1163 E−9 (0.4410)
Imports Australia	0.002619 (1.6494)	0.006386 (2.3623)	0.002079 (3.3547)	0.000750 (0.4483)
Imports Australia squared	—	−0.4170 E−7 (0.1964)	—	0.2058 E−6 (1.2529)
Imports Canada	−0.001787 (1.1903)	0.004333 (1.0187)	−0.001465 (−2.1814)	0.002770 (1.0719)
Imports Canada squared	—	−0.3076 E−6 (0.8071)	—	−0.2649 E−6 (1.0464)
Imports Finland	0.017046 (1.1120)	0.058938 (1.4769)	—	—
Imports Finland squared	—	0.3158E−4 (1.4125)	—	—
Exports USA	−0.000565 (1.8400)	0.001250 (2.1411)	−0.000154 (1.2150)	0.000484 (1.3439)
Exports USA squared	—	−0.2057 E−7 (2.8521)	—	−0.4840 E−8 (1.1912)
Exports EEC	0.000124 (0.8075)	0.000682 (2.7150)	0.000024 (0.4150)	0.2497 E−5 (0.0266)
Exports EEC squared	—	−0.8750 E−9 (1.7342)	—	0.4915 E−10 (0.2493)
Exports Australia	0.000465 (0.2377)	−0.007768 (2.0526)	−0.001245 (1.2684)	0.000519 (0.2225)
Exports Australia squared	—	0.6471 E−6 (1.7214)	—	−0.2492 E−6 (1.2573)
Exports Canada	0.002290 (1.2152)	−0.000816 (0.1456)	0.002133 (2.3309)	−.002433 (0.5798)
Exports Canada squared	—	0.4541 E−6 (0.7784)	—	0.4721 E−6 (1.0388)

(*continued*)

Table 4.2 (continued)

Exogenous variables	Initiated cases (1980–1987)		Affirmed cases (1980–1986)	
	(1)	(2)	(3)	(4)
Exports Finland	−0.003934	−0.012050		
	(1.3798)	(2.1858)	—	—
Exports Finland squared	—	−0.1342 E−5 (1.9670)	—	—
Real personal GDP	0.000994 (1.5830)	0.001038 (2.3573)	0.000543 (1.5974)	0.000502 (1.5975)
Constant	0.094559 (0.0224)	−7.054138 (2.2257)	−1.10796 (0.4861)	−3.081474 (1.3528)
Adjusted R^2 =	.7529	.8901	.7243	.7774

Table 4.3 Explaining the number of initiated anti-dumping cases by the individual country bringing the complaint (absolute t-statistics in parentheses)

Exogenous variables	United States	EEC	Australia	Canada	Finland
	(1)	(2)	(3)	(4)	(5)
Nonmarket dummy	3.43955 (2.2615)	12.95112 (6.5296)	0.65498 (0.3956)	1.20800 (0.4880)	1.52672 (4.5128)
Imports	0.00014 (1.5917)	−0.15050 (1.7662)	0.00240 (4.5203)	−0.00075 (1.5831)	0.00130 (0.9730)
Imports squared	−0.609 E−9 (3.1320)	0.126 E−9 (0.7830)	−0.262 E−7 (3.4263)	0.625 E−7 (2.0039)	−.426 E−6 (0.9537)
Exports	0.810 E−4 (0.9596)	0.000176 (2.2781)	0.00129 (2.3970)	0.00190 (2.9261)	−0.000137 (0.5100)
Exports squared	0.108 E−9 (0.6531)	−0.165 E−9 (1.2271)	−0.364 E−7 (3.1498)	−0.983 E−7 (2.0444)	0.135 E−8 (0.0764)
Real personal GDP	0.00014 (0.8247)	0.00062 (2.6028)	0.00029 (1.4913)	0.659 E−5 (0.04098	0.500 E−4 (1.2819)
Constant	−0.27700 (0.2290)	−1.5288 (0.9565)	−1.36215 (1.0785)	0.85992 (0.8162)	−0.28395 (1.0994)
Adjusted R^2 =	.7259	.4753	.8394	.7241	.2335

ket economies, though the coefficients are not significant for Australia and Canada in table 4.3. The results are also economically important. When each country's data are plugged into these regressions, it is possible to estimate how many anti-dumping cases were brought against each country because of its nonmarket nature. For example, the first specification in table 4.2 implies that of the predicted 21.7

dumping cases initiated against Bulgarian exporters, 20.3 (or 93.7 percent) were attributable to those firms' government-owned status. Similarly, the shares of predicted dumping complaints against the other nine nonmarket economies that can be explained by their form of market organization are: China (43.3%), Czechoslovakia (71.5%), the German Democratic Republic (65.4%), Hungary (76.1%), North Korea (83.9%), Poland (68.0%), Romania (64.6%), the Soviet Union (65.8%), and Yugoslavia (72.2%).

With regard to the other variables in regression (1), higher imports usually imply that more dumping cases will be filed, and this effect is also often quite significant. The evidence for exports is somewhat more mixed, with this variable entering both positively and negatively in tables 4.2 and 4.3's regressions. The mixed coefficient signs suggest that a desire to avoid future retaliation against trade actions may not be the only link between exports and dumping investigations.[23] The fact that the squared terms for the import and export variables often enter significantly (again with varying signs) indicates that the relationship between trade flows and dumping complaints is nonlinear. Finally, the coefficient for real per capita GDP is often significant, and its positive sign implies that just as less developed countries are granted lower tariff rates for many of their exports, the probability that dumping charges will be brought against their exports also is lower.

Next, these regressions were rerun with two changes: (1) only anti-dumping cases with affirmative decisions are examined, and (2) the observations for Finland were dropped because of the unavailability of data on the number of affirmative cases for that country. The estimation results for affirmative anti-dumping decisions are reported in columns 3 and 4 of table 4.2 (for the pooled regressions) and table 4.4 (for the individual country regressions).

As in the first regressions, dumping complaints are consistently affirmed at higher rates against nonmarket economies than they are against market economies, though the coefficients are again not significant for Australia and Canada in table 4.4.[24] Again, the regression results are also economically significant. Using the linear specification in table 4.2 implies that of the predicted 12.2 dumping cases successfully brought against Bulgarian exporters, 12.3 (or 100.8 percent) were attributable to those firms' government-owned status. For the nine other nonmarket countries, the corresponding percentage of their predicted affirmative dumping decisions that can be explained by their form of market organization are: China (54.1%), Czechoslo-

Table 4.4 Explaining the number of affirmed anti-dumping cases by the individual country bringing the complaint (Absolute t-statistics in parentheses)

Exogenous variables	United States (1)	EEC (2)	Australia (3)	Canada (4)
Nonmarket dummy	2.25662 (2.4053)	7.35900 (6.6010)	0.61832 (0.7444)	1.11367 (1.3112)
Imports	0.00010 (2.0256)	−0.713 E−4 (1.8450)	0.001435 (5.8312)	−0.00040 (1.8533)
Imports squared	−0.312 E−9 (2.4832)	0.116 E−9 (1.4094)	−0.216 E−7 (5.3040)	0.596 E−7 (3.5445)
Exports	0.556 E−4 (1.2829)	0.818 E−4 (2.4826)	0.00041 (1.6456)	0.00160 (4.3688)
Exports squared	−0.989 E−10 (1.0758)	−0.125 E−9 (2.1605)	−0.870 E−8 (1.3631)	−0.110 E−6 (3.6109)
Real personal GDP	0.401 E−4 (0.3740)	0.00045 (3.4160)	0.770 E−4 (0.7906)	−0.207 E−4 (0.2161)
Constant	−0.10856 (0.1446)	−1.6448 (1.8144)	−0.35084 (0.5539)	0.24894 (0.3902)
Adjusted R^2 =	.5776	.5028	.8252	.7211

vakia (79.4%), the German Democratic Republic (74.2%), Hungary (83.4%), North Korea (92.5%), Poland (82.7%), Romania (72.2%), the Soviet Union (67.4%), and Yugoslavia (79.2%). Notably, for each country the effect of market organization is even more pronounced among affirmative investigations than it is for cases that are simply initiated.

As with the initiated cases, higher imports and exports are usually associated with more affirmative dumping decisions, and the relationship between trade flows and dumping disputes is usually nonlinear. The coefficient for real per capita GDP is consistently positive (except for Canada), supporting the hypothesis that preferential treatment is granted to less developed trading partners to encourage exports and promote economic development.

A skeptical reader will undoubtedly be concerned by the unavoidable use of the proxy variables (particularly for nonmarket economies) along with their inherent measurement error. The model is thus underidentified since the set of maximum-likelihood solutions contains more than one point. However, as long as the K reverse regressions all yield estimates of the same sign for each variable as in the direct regression, the interval between the maximum and minimum values for a coefficient from this (K + 1) set of estimates will contain

the true coefficient (Koopmans 1937). The problem is further complicated by the proxy variables being assumed to differ from their true
values by measurement error and some unknown scaling factor d. As
long as the sign of d is known, however, only the sign of the true coefficient can be inferred, which is this chapter's real concern (Leamer
1978, 237–245). Unfortunately, the minimum and maximum values
for these coefficient estimates for either columns 1 or 3 in table 4.2
are not bounded.[25]

Klepper and Leamer (1982) suggest one solution to this estimation
problem, which is to introduce additional information on the size of
the R^2 that one would observe if all the measurement error were
removed. The lower one's estimate of the model's explanatory power
in the absence of measurement error, the more likely it is that the
coefficient estimates can be bounded. Following Klepper and Leamer's lead, as long as R^{*2}—the R^2 obtained with this model assuming
no measurement error—is less than R_m^{*2}—the maximum value of R^{*2}
consistent with all of the normalized regressions in the same or-
thant—the parameter estimates will be bounded.[26] For columns 1 and
3 in table 4.2, the values for R_m^{*2} are .976 and .972. Thus, as long as
the reader believes that the model in the absence of measurement
error would not explain more than 97 percent of the variation in
the total number of initiated or affirmed dumping actions, the results
are not affected by either measurement errors or proxy variable
problems.[27]

As noted earlier, firms in nonmarket economies might have been
investigated and cited for dumping more frequently than their counterparts in market economies for reasons unrelated to their actual
pricing behavior. It is thus necessary to take another step to expunge
the effects of any potential systematic political biases. The two sections that follow undertake this task by testing whether defense-
related competition or differences in export composition across countries can account for tables 4.2–4.4's results.[28]

B. Examining the Political Motives for Charging Firms with Dumping

If systematic biases do exist against nonmarket firms in terms of either the rate of enforcement or the methods by which below-cost
pricing is determined, one must still explain why the agency officials
who administer anti-dumping procedures would want to make systematic mistakes in evaluating predation from just one group of
countries. It is surely conceivable that bureaucrats in market econo-

mies are relatively more hostile to nonmarket economies. However, if this political bias produces systematic discrimination against nonmarket economies, the returns to this discrimination and therefore its level should vary across countries.

One important political influence that may affect anti-dumping proceedings stems from defense-related competition with nonmarket countries. Presumably, the United States—which led the fight to prevent technology transfers to communist countries and frequently lobbied Western Europe to increase defense expenditures—would also have had the greatest return to bringing up defense-related dumping charges.[29] Because of free-riding problems the United States (the largest country and thus the one best able to internalize investments in the West's defense) should have imposed the largest penalties on nonmarket economies. Likewise, the nonaligned countries with the lowest returns to competing militarily with communist countries should also have been the least concerned with imposing trade sanctions on nonmarket countries. Finally, countries allied with the United States should fall in between these two extremes.[30]

To test this hypothesis, I pooled together time series and cross-sectional data on the number of dumping investigations undertaken by Australia, Austria, Canada, the EEC, Finland, Spain, Sweden, and the United States from 1980 to 1987 against firms in market and nonmarket economies.[31] The dependent variable is now the number of anti-dumping cases that a country initiated against exporters from nonmarket economies in a given year. Besides the country imposing the sanctions, the regressions also control for the total number of investigations by that country and for the value of exports and imports between the investigating country and its nonmarket trading partners. Regression (2) is specified as:

$$\begin{aligned}
INITIATED \; & AGAINST \; NONMARKET_{i,t} = a_0 \\
& + a_1 \; EUROPEANS \; WITHOUT \; U.S. \; DEFENSE \; TREATY_{i,t} \\
& + a_2 \; UNITED \; STATES_{i,t} \\
& + a_3 \; EUROPEANS \; WITH \; U.S. \; DEFENSE \; TREATY_{i,t} \quad (2) \\
& + a_4 \; NONMARKET \; IMPORTS_{i,t} \\
& + a_5 \; NONMARKET \; EXPORTS_{i,t} \\
& + a_6 \; TOTAL \; NUMBER \; INITIATED_{i,t} + \sum_{t=1981}^{1987} a_t \; YEAR_t + u_{i,t}
\end{aligned}$$

In order to test how the political returns to imposing economic sanctions vary across countries, the regressions include three different dummy variables. *EUROPEANS WITHOUT U.S. DEFENSE TREATY*$_{i,t}$ is a dummy that equals one if the country does not have a defense pact with the United States (i.e., Austria, Finland, and Sweden) and zero otherwise. To allow for the possibility that the United States's political interests are not perfectly aligned with those of its defense allies, I used a separate dummy for the U.S., *UNITED STATES*$_{i,t}$. EUROPEANS WITH U.S. DEFENSE TREATY$_{i,t}$ is a dummy for the Western-aligned nations of Europe (i.e., the EEC and Spain). I also included year dummies for 1981–1987, *YEAR*$_t$. The intercept thus represents Australia and Canada in 1980. In some years several countries did not initiate any anti-dumping cases, and because of this, all four specifications were estimated as tobit regressions. Table 4.5 reports the normalized coefficient values from those regressions.[32]

The results strongly reject the hypothesis that dumping complaints are motivated by defense-related political concerns. In the first three specifications, the hypothesis that the coefficients for the United States and nonaligned countries dummies are essentially the same.[33] Even if we were to accept the coefficients' values as the true ones, the differences in rates of investigation are economically small. The results in columns (1) and (2) indicate that had the United States behaved as the nonaligned countries did, it would have brought between 2.7 and 4.0 fewer cases against nonmarket firms over the eight-year period. This represents only 7.7 to 11.4 percent of the total number of nonmarket cases that the United States actually brought between 1980 and 1987. Column (3) actually indicates that the United States was the *least* likely to bring cases, and that it would have brought 4.9 more cases (14.0%) against nonmarket firms than it actually did if it had behaved like the nonaligned countries. In the fourth specification, which provides the best fit for the data, the hypothesis that there is no difference in the countries' rates of investigation is rejected at the 5 percent level. And contrary to the defense theory, the regressions imply that the United States was actually *less* likely than nonaligned countries to bring dumping charges against nonmarket firms.[34] The results indicate that if the U.S. behaved like the nonaligned nations in the sample, it would have brought 8.5 additional cases, a 24.3 percent increase, against nonmarket firms.

The defense hypothesis was inconsistent with the results for the Western European nations with United States defense agreements which were consistently, though not statistically significantly, less

Table 4.5 Does the number of cases initiated against nonmarket economies differ across countries for political reasons? (Tobit estimation. Absolute t-statistics in parentheses.)

Exogenous variables	Endogenous variable: Number of cases brought against nonmarket economies			
	(1)	(2)	(3)	(4)
Europeans without U.S.	−0.9294	−0.7932	−0.8752	0.4609
Defense treaty dummy	(1.462)	(1.149)	(1.196)	(0.537)
Europeans with U.S.	−1.4380	−1.3642	−1.3460	−0.1599
Defense treaty dummy	(1.493)	(1.304)	(0.999)	(0.111)
United States dummy	−0.2391	−0.2647	−1.9374	−1.7960
	(0.519)	(0.570)	(2.565)	(2.235)
Total number of	0.0188	0.0250	0.0234	0.0503
initiated cases	(1.873)	(2.058)	(2.267)	(3.523)
Imports from nonmarket	0.224 E−3	0.228 E−3	0.201 E−3	−0.128 E−3
economies	(2.707)	(2.642)	(1.090)	(0.556)
Imports from nonmarket	—	—	−0.208 E−8	0.545 E−8
economies squared			(0.500)	(1.035)
Exports to nonmarket	−0.116 E−3	−0.111 E−3	0.416 E−3	0.759 E−3
economies	(1.413)	(1.284)	(2.277)	(3.442)
Exports to nonmarket	—	—	−0.122 E−7	−0.204 E−7
economies squared			(3.222)	(4.264)
1981	—	1.4928	—	1.6658
		(2.231)		(2.295)
1982	—	0.2107	—	−0.7943
		(0.273)		(0.924)
1983	—	0.5403	—	0.4319
		(0.778)		(0.576)
1984	—	1.2611		1.3841
		(1.772)		(1.792)
1985	—	0.9720	—	0.8677
		(1.384)		(1.109)
1986	—	0.9284	—	1.3639
		(1.376)		(1.714)
1987	—	0.8429	—	1.7129
		(1.273)		(2.184)
Constant	−0.3337	−1.3508	−1.5483	−3.9989
	(0.597)	(1.778)	(2.310)	(3.735)
Log likelihood function =	−112.61	−108.56	−104.75	−97.22

likely to initiate such cases than were nonaligned countries. The defense theory is also inconsistent with the finding that, with one exception, Australia and Canada were always the most likely to bring nonmarket investigations. Given that defense-related political motives do not appear to underlie the United States' or Western Europe's anti-dumping investigations, it is difficult to believe that such a stance would hold for Australia and Canada.

C. Dumping and Political Protection from Competition

A second possible political bias could arise if nonmarket exports were concentrated in those industries receiving the greatest aggregate protection under the anti-dumping laws in the importing country. Certain industries may be more successful than others in obtaining protection from foreign competition.[35] The central question is whether the pattern of anti-dumping protection across industries was positively correlated with the share of the investigating countries' imports accounted for by nonmarket firms. If these variables were positively correlated, nonmarket enterprises might be charged with or found guilty of dumping more frequently than firms in market economies simply because of differences in the composition of their exports.

This hypothesis was tested using two different data sets. First, I calculated the share of developed market economies' imports of agricultural products, textiles, metals and basic products, chemicals and all other products accounted for by nonmarket exporters. I also calculated the fraction of developed market economies' total anti-dumping cases that fell into each of these five product groups. Both sets of data were available for 1979–1982, and they are reported in Panel A of table 4.6. The Pearson correlation coefficient between these two variables is -0.585, but is significant only at the 30.6 percent level. Panel B shows a similar breakdown for anti-dumping actions brought by the United States in eight categories between 1980 and 1986, with a Pearson correlation coefficient of -0.332.

Both sets of findings allow us to strongly reject the argument that nonmarket enterprises are more frequently investigated or cited for dumping merely because of the product composition of their exports to market economies. In fact, the negative correlations in table 4.6 suggest that the estimates provided in section III(A) may *understate* the true effect of market organization on a country's propensity to engage in below-cost pricing abroad.

Table 4.6   Are the products that nonmarket economies export more heavily protected from competition?

Panel A. All Market Economies (1979–1982)

Product class	% of total anti-dumping actions by market economies	% of developed market economy imports from nonmarket economy firms
Agriculture	4.61	9.50
Textiles	5.70	5.45
Metals	41.50	5.12
Chemicals	22.33	4.12
Other	25.85	4.75

Pearson correlation coefficient = −0.585 (30.6% significance level)

SOURCES: United Nations Conference on Trade and Development, *Handbook of International Trade and Development Statistics* (1981, 1984, 1985, table A), and United Nations Conference on Trade and Development, *Problems of Protectionism and Structural Adjustment* (1984, table 5).

Panel B. United States (1980–1986)

Product class	% of total anti-dumping actions by United States	% of United States imports from nonmarket economy firms
Food and beverage, animal and vegetable oils	5.1	2.9
Crude materials and fuels	5.0	1.4
Chemicals and pharmaceuticals	11.1	3.0
Manufactured goods classified by chief material except textiles and steel	5.14	2.1
Iron and steel	59.0	0.9
Textiles and apparel	4.1	6.8
Machinery, equipment and transport equipment	7.8	0.2
Miscellaneous manufacturing	3.0	2.1

Pearson correlation coefficient = −0.332 (42.3% significance level)

SOURCES: United Nations, *1986 International Trade Statistics Yearbook,* Volume 1 (1988, special table B) and Brown and Haas-Wilson 1990, table 4.

NOTES: Import data are for 1983.

D. Some Biases in the Data

The data have three biases that work toward finding relatively fewer dumping complaints being lodged against nonmarket economies. First, while the only type of dumping cases lodged against nonmarket economies involved below-cost sales, cases brought against market economies include both instances of below-cost pricing and price discrimination.[36] This biases the results against finding that nonmarket economies engage more frequently in below-cost pricing than do market economies. In fact, where it was possible to partially disaggregate the data, only 15 percent of the dumping cases initiated in 1987 by the United States against exporters from market economies employed evidence on below-cost pricing (United States International Trade Commission 1987 and Federal Register, various issues in 1987). Unfortunately, however, bringing a case on price discrimination grounds does not rule out that below-cost pricing was also occurring. Investigations analyze cost information only if the benchmark price used in demonstrating price discrimination is viewed as unreliable. Thus, the statistic of 15 percent provides only a lower bound on how much the results in section III(A) have overestimated the number of cases brought against market economies, but it does indicate that the bias against finding that government enterprises engage in "predatory-like" behavior may be quite important.

The second bias was that, while private corporations do not operate in nonmarket economies, many government enterprises do exist in market economies. The theory that government enterprises are more likely to engage in below-cost pricing implies that using the difference in the number of dumping cases brought against the two different types of economies provides a downwardly biased estimate of the difference in rates at which private and government corporations engage in below-cost pricing. Again, using the dumping cases initiated by the United States against market economies in 1987, only two of the thirty complaints against market economies explicitly noted that the firms against which the complaints were filed were owned by foreign governments. The three government-owned enterprises in these two cases were located in Israel, France, and Belgium. Thus, while the estimates of the likelihood of nonmarket organizations being charged with dumping are biased downward, the evidence suggests that the bias against finding "predatory-like" behavior by government enterprises is not particularly large.

Finally, excluding all countervailing duty cases (and not just those brought against market economies) biases the reported results *against* finding predatory behavior by government enterprises. The anti-dumping laws provide legal remedies against anti-competitive export pricing that is not directly motivated by a government's industrial or trade policies. Because firms in nonmarket economies are government-owned, the line between subsidized exports and below-cost exports is blurred. A possible objection to focusing upon anti-dumping charges, therefore, is that some disputes involve subsidized exports, and they are normally brought under the countervailing duty laws. Such cases may be brought as dumping actions against nonmarket firms, thereby systematically biasing the data. However, there are two good reasons to believe that this bias does not exist. First, even if the dumping cases in the sample include some instances where nonmarket firms charged low prices as a result of receiving government subsidies, those cases should be included in my measure of dumping. There is no analytical distinction between a parent company providing a subsidy to one of its subsidiaries which then engages in below-cost pricing and incurs losses, and a government subsidizing its enterprise for the purpose of engaging in below-cost pricing. Second, subsidies are treated legally as distinct from private pricing behavior for both market and nonmarket firms.[37] Countervailing duty cases have in fact been brought against firms in nonmarket economies (see Finger and Olechowski 1987, 260–263).[38]

IV. Summary

The technical analysis of this chapter has been quite complicated, but the results obtained are important and reinforce the earlier findings in this book. Economic theory and empirical evidence have both suggested that government-owned enterprises tend to be motivated more by goals such as output, employment, or revenue maximization than by strict profit maximization. The evidence confirms the hypothesis that government enterprises find it less costly than profit-maximizing firms to engage in below-cost pricing. The economic importance of the effect is quite large—between 43 and 94 percent of initiated below-cost sales dumping cases and between 54 and 100 percent of affirmative dumping decisions against exporting firms from nonmarket economies are attributable to those firms' government-owned status. This result cannot simply be explained away by political biases against nonmarket economies in anti-dumping procedures. To the contrary, after controlling for possible biases from military-related political competition, the empirical work shows that in some cases the United States would have brought nearly one-fourth more dumping cases against nonmarket firms had it behaved like the non-aligned countries in the sample. The results are also robust when possible political biases stemming from the industry composition of non-market exports are controlled for. Again, this bias implies that the above results may understate the true effect of market organization on a country's propensity to engage in below-cost pricing abroad.

Just as many economists believe, with some justification, that the government often brings antitrust cases when the evidence does not warrant intervention, dumping may indeed not be as prevalent as government charges indicate. I am quite willing to accept that conclusion. However, as long as one accepts that some portion of the dumping cases was justified and that firms from nonmarket countries are not systematically discriminated against, the evidence implies that firms in nonmarket economies engage in predatory behavior at a higher rate than private enterprises. The evidence presented here suggests that governments around the world view government enterprises as posing a much greater predatory threat than do private firms.

FIVE

What Happens When the Victims Have Better Information Than the Predators?

Gould's abilities lay largely in the field of corporate negotiation and security trading . . . Sometimes his interests in a corporation were primary; often his stock market interests were primary, and he used his position on the board to further his stock speculations. In still other cases, he had a continuous interest in both his capacities.
(Grodinsky 1957, 22)

So wrote the biographer of Jay Gould (1836–1892), describing the financier's practice of integrating his business strategies with stock market trading strategies. As I document below, Gould would often use information from his own business decisions to make profits from trading in his own firms' securities *and in competing firms' securities.* While trading in one's own firm's securities would now be illegal in the United States, it is legal today to use private information to guide one's trading in *other* firm's securities. This chapter will examine how information resulting from a business decision made by one company can be used to make trading profits in another company's securities, and how these trading profits affect the economics of the original business decision.

More important, this discussion will show how sensitive the traditional game-theoretic discussions of predation are to adopting very special assumptions about the information possessed by potential entrants. This chapter focuses on the case of entry: if entry will reduce the market value of an incumbent firm, how does the opportunity for making trading profits affect the entry decision, and how does it affect the ability of the incumbent to deter entry via a low price/predation strategy? My central assumption is that potential entrants have the best information on whether they are going to enter a market. The idea is of more than theoretical/historical interest, which I will illustrate through a modern business event involving both business and securities trading strategies.

For over twenty years, the Polaroid Corporation enjoyed a classic monopoly position in the business of instant photography. After reaching its all-time high in 1970, Polaroid's market value began declining, and by 1974 its total value had fallen by a little over 2 billion dollars. Many factors might explain this tremendous decline in value, but one factor that must be considered is the entry of Eastman Kodak into the instant photography market. While Kodak's entry had been anticipated as early as 1970, Kodak did not announce the development of its own instant photography system until 1974. On the day of the announcement, Polaroid's stock fell by 10 ⅛ points—from 79 ⅝ to 69 ½, a more than $300 million drop in Polaroid's market value—while Kodak's stock increased by 2 ⅛ to 110 ⅞. On that same day, publicly traded call options on Polaroid's stock fell by almost 50 percent: for instance, an option to buy Polaroid shares at $80 in July 1974 traded at 9 ⅜ the day before Kodak's announcement and at 5 ¼ the day after.

Apparently, Kodak's decision to enter Polaroid's market reduced Polaroid's market value substantially. Since Kodak knew about its entry decision before anybody else, the question arises as to why Kodak should not have taken advantage of its superior information by trading in Polaroid's securities.[1] Kodak could have sold Polaroid stock short before its entry announcements, or it could have written and sold call options before the announcements and then bought those options back at lower prices on subsequent days.[2] Or, instead of the company entering into such transactions itself, Kodak's managers could have made the trade for their own accounts, or Kodak could have passed the information on to others (e.g., its investment bankers) who could have profited. Then, just as today, there were no legal restrictions that prohibited Kodak from profiting on information relating to Polaroid's stock value. Insider trading laws do not specifically prevent the trading in one company's stock by another company.[3] Also, there are no legal restrictions on how much of a company can be short-sold by one individual. (This can be compared to the 13-D and antitrust restrictions that come into play when a company takes a *long* position in another company's stock). If these trading strategies somehow seem distasteful, consider one other way that Kodak could have profited from its information: what if the manager of Kodak's *pension fund* knew about Kodak's discovery and decision? Then instead of holding Polaroid stock in the portfolio in proportion to its market value (as the Capital Asset Pricing Model prescribes), the portfolio manager could have simply *reduced* his holding of Polaroid. His portfolio would then show a return in excess of the market's, even without a short position in Polaroid.

If Kodak stood to gain profits from changes in Polaroid stock value arising from Kodak's entry decision, how would this "trading profit" have affected Kodak's entry decisions? Intuitively, trading profits seem to produce additional potential benefits from entry and therefore should promote entry.

Another question involves how trading profits affect the ability of an incumbent firm such as Polaroid to practice entry deterrence. Suppose, for example, that Polaroid had committed itself to higher outputs to deter Kodak from entering. Upon Kodak's entry, these higher outputs would have translated into even lower profits for Polaroid (the standard predation story), and therefore Polaroid's stock value would have dropped even more than if it had not attempted to deter entry. However, if Kodak had a short position in Polaroid stock, Polaroid's losses translate into trading profits for Kodak and encourage entry. This argument—that the predator hurts itself more than the entrant because it must expand output and lower price—reinforces the true difficulty of successfully deterring new entry by ignoring trading profits.

While the Kodak/Polaroid case illustrates the general point of how distributive effects from trading profits can change the economics of entry and entry deterrence, the focus of this discussion is more complicated. The preceding discussion suggests only that trading profits increase the likelihood of entry and decrease the profitability of entry deterrence, yet this might not generally be true since there is another way to make trading profits: a potential entrant could decide *not to enter* while simultaneously taking a *long position* in the incumbent's stock. (Think of what would have happened to Polaroid's stock price if Kodak in 1974 had credibly announced that it would not enter Polaroid's market.) The trading profits from the long position/no entry strategy become an opportunity cost of entry; whether the trading profits from the short position outweigh the long position depends upon, (1) the relative ability of the entrant to profit from decreases in the incumbent's value versus increases in the incumbent's value, and (2) the expectations of the capital market concerning the *ex ante* probability of entry.

The incumbent/predator in modern theories of entry deterrence and predation has proprietary information on its costs. In contrast, I focus on the naturally privileged position enjoyed by the entrant over his own entry decision and on how the potential for trading profits depends upon this asymmetry. My central finding is that trading profits have a "smoothing" effect on the probability of entry: they increase the probability of entry when entry is *ex ante* unlikely and decrease the probability of entry when entry is *ex ante* likely. The reasons for this smoothing lie in how the incumbent's share price reacts to the potential entrant's behavior. If entry were *ex ante* considered unlikely, there would be a large movement in the incumbent's share price if entry did occur, so trading profits from the short position/enter strategy would be relatively large and entry would be encouraged. On the other hand, if entry were considered *ex ante* likely, trading profits from the long position/no enter strategy would be relatively large and entry would be encouraged. Entry deterrence faces the same smoothing result. If in the absence of trading profits an incumbent is very successful at entry deterrence (meaning that the probability of entry is close to zero), trading profits will make entry deterrence less profitable and the incumbent will be less likely to engage in the activity. Likewise, trading profits may make previously unsuccessful deterrence more successful.

While there is a certain asymmetry in the valuation effects of entering versus not entering, as noted below, certain laws regulate long positions in companies (especially competitors) so there is some reason to believe that a potential entrant can more easily profit from decreases in an incumbent's value. (Long position profits or buying call options are also somewhat precarious because a potential entrant must convince the capital market that it will never enter the market, something that is hard to do credibly. It is easier to surprise the market by announcing entry.)

The analysis presented here is a simple extension of Hirshleifer's (1971) observation that inventors can internalize the value of their discoveries by trading in assets whose prices will probably change after disclosure of the discovery. Unfortunately, Hirshleifer's important insight has been relegated to footnotes in the sections of industrial organization texts that deal with R&D and patents. My analysis shows that distributive effects are present in a much wider variety of situations than R&D and that they can change the predictions of economic models. But clearly, distributive effects are present in virtually any strategic situation (e.g., auctions and oligopoly), so many economic models would have to be altered if firms could avail themselves of the opportunity to obtain these trading profits.

This analysis has implications for other areas and brings a new view to certain public policy issues. First, this analysis holds only if the incumbent firm has publicly traded stock; it follows that firms whose stock is not publicly traded enjoy certain competitive advantages since their competitors cannot supplement profits from competitive strategies with trading profits. Nontraded companies should therefore be more common in situations where it is particularly important to prevent entry.[4]

Second, trading profits are less risky if the incumbent firm has only one line of business; this implies a new benefit to diversification—diversification makes it more difficult for competitors (and other persons who can deduce or affect a company's situation through their own business dealings) to make trading profits.[5] Third, from a public policy perspective insider trading regulations appear curiously inconsistent. If it is "bad" for company A to trade in its own securities using superior information, why is it not "bad" for company A to trade in the securities of company B, if company A has superior information on the value of B?[6]

Fourth, the legal treatment of long and short positions also appears inconsistent: if an investor accumulates 5 percent of a company's stock, it must report that. In contrast, there are currently no reporting requirements on short positions, though there is now a movement to require the reporting of large short positions. If my analysis of trading profits is correct, an efficiency explanation for existing reporting requirements as well as insider trading rules may rest on the effect they have on corporations' competitive strategies. Finally, while both firms and their workers have an interest in corporate pension funds being run in-house since there is a likelihood that the pension fund managers will get information relevant to the value of other companies' securities, the question remains as to whether such an arrangement promotes overall financial market efficiency.

My discussion focuses on the effects that stock trading profits have on the incentive to encourage or deter entry, yet the number of instances where one firm's actions can significantly influence the value of another firm's securities seems endless (e.g., the settlement negotiations between Texaco and Pennzoil or the decision by airlines to order Boeing jets). Acquisitions are often associated with insider trading, and the evidence that acquisitions affect the share prices of other competitors is also well documented (e.g., Stillman 1983). This chapter's discussion implies that selling short the stocks of third-party firms can increase the incentive for firms to go through with efficiency-creating mergers.

Another recent analysis by Robert Hansen and myself (1996) carries this discussion of interdependencies between firms a step further. It shows that, besides the assumption employed here that companies impose externalities on one another, only one other assumption is necessary to make nonvalue-maximizing behavior the desired policy of shareholders: that shareholders own diversified portfolios. Any kind of externality, pecuniary or nonpecuniary, vertical or horizontal, will suffice. What matters is simply that one company's actions affect another's value. Diversification therefore offers additional benefits to shareholders (internalization of externalities) besides the traditional benefit of risk reduction. However, we also found that the private incentives to deviate from a diversified portfolio are greater than previously recognized. An interesting question that therefore emerges is whether institutional arrangements have arisen to enforce diversification and prevent individual shareholders from imposing costs upon others through value-maximizing behavior.

The next section examines three specific instances where these types of trading patterns were successfully used. Section III addresses the legal issues concerning the types of financial transactions that we envision. Section IV presents formal models, first one of entry with a passive incumbent and then one with an entry-deterring incumbent. Finally, the chapter concludes with a brief summary and a discussion of implications.

II. Recorded Incidents of the Practice

All the examples here concern the business dealings of Jay Gould, although in one instance it was Gould's competitor who was profiting from changes in the value of a Gould company stock. The focus is on Gould only because Hansen and I first found documentation of his following the practice. I suspect that investigations of the other "robber barons" of the late nineteenth and early twentieth centuries would turn up further instances. I have not found any modern instances of the practice and do not know if this is because of a simple lack of documentation (it is the type of behavior that one would not want to publicize) or a lack of opportunities (as noted below, businesses like railroads and steamship lines are particularly susceptible to the practice); or because modern institutions like company-run pension funds provide an alternative method of profiting from changes in competitors' values.[7] The desire not to publicize short selling of a competitor's stock may simply reflect the fear that such trading will be detected and thus signal the company's competitive strategy (see also Carlton and Fischel 1983, 885).[8]

A. Gould and the Western Union

In the late 1870s, Jay Gould demonstrated a mastery at acquiring and merging railroad systems. Looking further, Gould saw the tremendous synergies between railroads and telegraphs. "The telegraph and the railroad systems go hand in hand, as it were, integral parts of a great civilization," he stated. "I naturally became acquainted with the telegraph business and gradually became interested in it. I thought well of it as an investment, and I kept increasing my interests" (quoted in Josephson 1934, 205). However, Western Union, the dominant telegraph company in the country at that time, had no interest in allowing Gould to have a position on its board of directors (Josephson, 205). Gould therefore resorted to building his own telegraph company. But he coupled his business strategy with a financial strategy of shorting Western Union stock:

> Forming an alliance with the stock market "wizard," James Keene, and other speculators, Gould began "shorting" Western Union; and soon the bears won a million a piece at this destructive operation, while the owners grew consternated. But as if this were not enough, the wily little man, with the advice of a technician, a certain General Eckert, set about building a telegraph line of his own along the tracks of his railroads, which he named the "Atlantic and Pacific Company" ... Soon he had cut heavily into his opponents' business, which declined $2,000,000 in one year. (Josephson, 205)

While the Western Union ended up buying the Atlantic and Pacific Company from Gould, this did not satisfy Gould's appetite for the telegraph business (or perhaps it just did not eliminate the potential profits to be had from further entry). Gould then acquired the American Union, a telegraph company to which his existing and newly acquired railroads energetically switched their contracts, previously made with the Western Union (Grodinsky 1957, 275). Gould again used trading profits from short-selling Western Union stock to complement his profits from running American Union. Joining with others whom he had convinced "that with the American Union becoming ever more aggressive, the Western Union earnings were bound to decline," Gould and his group built up "a large short interest" (Grodinsky , 276).[9] Western Union's profitability was seriously eroded.[10] In the end, Gould finally ended up making "millions of [dollars] profits on the short side" and eventually took control of Western Union (Josephson, 206). While selling the shares of Western Union short, he had been buying its proxies. These proxies traded separately from the stock itself and helped give Gould the ability to vote himself into power.

B. Gould, Park, the Pacific Mail and the Panama Transit Company

Gould's biographer describes an exploit of one of Gould's competitors: "According to one story, published many years after the event, by an observer who had apparently unusual sources of information, Park is said to have sold 60,000 shares of Pacific Mail short in anticipation of the injury which a Panama-controlled steamship service would inflict upon the Pacific Mail" (Grodinsky, 147).

The original story appeared in the "By-the-Bye in Wall Street" column in the September 17, 1925 issue of the *Wall Street Journal* ("By-the-Bye" seems to have been the forerunner of today's "Heard on the Street" column). The story is told in a humorous style. By way of background, the Pacific Mail was a steamship line that transported goods between the east and west coasts of the United States via the Isthmus of Panama. Gould controlled the corporation (this was in 1875). At a shareholders' meeting, Gould refused to answer one shareholder's questions—those of Mr. Trenor W. Park—and instead slyly remarked: "A gentleman so gifted ought to have a steamship line of his own. Go get it."

Nothing happened for a few days, and then all of a sudden Pacific Mail stock was being sold actively and its price fell. Trenor Park was starting a steamship line:

> One morning celebrated with a smash. Entire capital stock seemed suddenly come to market. Explanation was in word from Trenor Park. "Mr. Jay Gould is being accommodated," he said. "There is to be a new steamship line."
>
> Supplement followed in the newspapers—advertisement announced sailings by the Panama Transit Co., touching at every Pacific Mail port, cutting every Pacific Mail rate.
>
> Stock Exchange quotations plumped more points downward. Mr. Gould was quoted scoffing. What he might do to childish invaders exalted the spirits of every horror yearner. The entire market fell into

nervous weakness—Park pressure, quoth the oracles. Pacific Mail rallied aggressively—Gould whips getting busy, vouchsafed the same oracles. (*WSJ*)

It appears that the Gould and Park forces were fighting to see whether Park with short positions could force Pacific Mail down while Gould with long positions was trying to force Pacific Mail up.[11] Who would win?

> Disclosure came that Park had bought a lot of second-hand ships— "the scrap heap of the Clyde Steamship Co.," commented Gould, whose market-moving claque hurrahed a boom to show how superior were zenith assets, power and trusteeships to pessimist pretensions. Sympathy was not widespread for Trenor Park, pinioned short of stock beneath the current price, earner of his own doom ... Along came another newspaper advertisement whose small type looked a mile high to some readers. All it said was that the Panama Railroad had made a new contract—thrown over Mr. Gould's Pacific Mail, signed up with Mr. Park's Panama Transit—Park ships thenceforth exclusively accommodated with transfer of traffic across the Isthmus—Pacific Mail's round-the-continent trade invited to vie in idleness with the Ancient Mariner's painted ship upon a painted ocean.
>
> What happened in the stock market was aplenty. Trenor W. Park covered 60,000 shares of short Pacific Mail leisurely under 20, sales made from the top all the way down. (*WSJ*)

In the end, Mr. Park's short positions and development of Panama Transit seem to have earned him a couple of million dollars,[12] while Gould (who eventually gained control of Panama Transit) ruefully regretted his rude remarks at the shareholders' meeting in the amount of about $1 million.[13]

These examples clearly exhibit an entrant profiting from the changes in value of an incumbent firm. In both cases, entrants sold short the incumbent's stock and then entered the industry—greatly reducing the incumbent's profits and by doing so reaping large profits for themselves.[14] It is interesting to note certain common features to the incidents: in each case, the incumbent was a (virtual) monopolist, was publicly traded, and was a company with only one line of business. All of these features made it easy for an entrant to make almost riskless trading profits by shorting the incumbent. I am not sure if Jay Gould took the same lessons away that I do: if you are going to be a monopolist threatened by entry, then by all means do not allow your stock to be publicly traded; but if that is not possible, then acquire some unrelated businesses so that a short position in your stock will be risky.

C. A Related Modern Incident

While I cannot provide modern instances of short selling which involve entry, there is some contemporary evidence that short selling a competitor's stock is still practiced today.[15] While trading in one's own firm's securities is illegal in the United States, it is still legal to use private information to guide trading in *other* firms' securities. One such purported instance involved the Dole Food Company and Chiquita. I was informed of this in a discussion I had with Alan Best, who headed short sales at Shearson Lehmann Brothers.[16] Mr. Best reported instances in which a rival company—"a banana company on the West Coast"—took a short position in Dole Food 's stock just prior to Dole's quarterly earnings announcement in October 1991 (which was unexpectedly poor so that the share price declined significantly).[17] When I contacted investor relations at Dole it was confirmed that they "had heard of such rumors" and that they "suspected" that the rival engaged in the trading was Chiquita.

Documentary evidence consistent with these statements exists: In 1991 Dole reported a third quarter drop in net income of 41 percent from a year earlier (*Wall Street Journal,* October 18, 1991, B9). Dole's stock price declined by $5.875 a share (or 14 percent) the day after the announcement, and the number of shares sold short increased dramatically immediately before the company's earnings announcement. Prior to August 1991 short selling in Dole's stock was zero, while in the months around the earnings announcement it was: 73,636 on August 15th, 128,958 on September 15th, 596,928 on October 15th, and, after the earnings announcement, 173,156 on November 15th. Besides the question of entry there are perfectly rational reasons why a rival would hold a short position in a competitor. For example, simply by being in the same industry as the rival, one receives good information on the industry's economic condition and therefore on the rival's likely earnings.[18]

Another related example concerns trading by a scientist, his lawyers, and certain CBS employees. The scientist was scheduled to appear on the CBS Evening News to discuss G. D. Searle & Co.'s NutraSweet product, and he knew that he would give a very critical evaluation. The scientist and his lawyer admitted to buying Searle put options prior to his appearance on CBS, but both maintain that such action was legal (the SEC did launch an investigation because of suspicious trading in Searle options, but I found no record of formal charges being brought) ["SEC Probe of Searle Options Raises Questions on Ethics, Inside Trades," *Wall Street Journal,* May 18, 1984]. This case is related to the trading profits idea in that the gains from these trading profits would have increased the scientist's return to producing research. It is possible that such trading profits could alter scientists' choice of research activities, just as I argue here that trading profits affect business decisions.[19]

III. Legal and Practical Issues

My hypothesis is that entrant firms are able to take advantage of their superior information by trading in the securities of the incumbent firm. A natural concern over such a policy is its legality: do insider trading or fraud laws prohibit trading in a competitor's stocks? It appears that the answer is no.

There are (at least) three legal theories on why trading with nonpublic material information should be illegal.[20] First, there is the fiduciary duty principle: insiders (corporate officers and directors) cannot trade in *their* company's securities when they possess material nonpublic information since this violates their fiduciary duties to their shareholders. Second, there is the misappropriation theory, which forbids the use of stolen (i.e., misappropriated) information for private gain. And third, there is the equality of information idea: any trading based on information not available to other market participants ought to be illegal.

Only the third legal theory would apply to the type of trading that I suggest. The fiduciary principle clearly does not apply to trading in a competitor's stock since the *entrant* and its officers owe no fiduciary duty to the *incumbent's* shareholders. The misappropriation theory would not seem to apply since the information concerning the entrant's strategy is legitimately owned by the firm.[21] The third principle, equality of information, clearly does apply; the entrant does possess material information that is not available to other traders.

Carlton and Fischel (1983, 874) provide an example in which an executive of a firm's key supplier sells short the stock of the downstream firm and then withholds delivery of critical supplies. Citing the U.S. Supreme Court's 1980 Chiarella decision, Carlton and Fischel argue that the executive would face "little fear of penalty from insider trading laws" because the executive of the supplier probably does not owe a "fiduciary duty to the shareholders of another firm." While their discussion is important because they recognize the legality of trading in another firm's stock based upon inside information, they do not apply the discussion to whether short selling a competitor's stock increases the returns to entering an industry.

The current state of insider trading law upholds only the fiduciary duty doctrine. The Supreme Court stated the law most succinctly in the Chiarella case: "When an allegation of fraud is based upon non-disclosure, there can be no fraud absent a duty to speak. We hold that a duty to disclose under §10(b) does not arise from the mere possession of nonpublic market information" (445 U.S. 222, at 235 (1980)).

Whether an executive of one firm may privately trade in another firm's stock based upon his inside information is more complicated than the preceding discussion indicates. In *United States v. O'Hagan,* the Supreme Court recently accepted the misappropriation theory.[22] Thus, unless a company explicitly permits using this information for private gain, allowing a company's managers, investment banker, or pension funds manager to trade on inside information may be illegal.

Most emphatically, however, the courts have not accepted the third principle, that of equal information for all participants. It would seem, therefore, that one firm trading in another firm's stock avoids both the misappropriation and fiduciary duty rules and thus is not subject to legal sanctions based on insider trading laws. General fraud laws would also not apply in this case. To prove fraudulent behavior, a plaintiff must generally show that misstatements or misrepresentations were made; simple withholding of relevant information is not enough (Barber 1987, 173).

Practical considerations could of course rule out this proposed trading schemes even if legal considerations did not. Specifically, the easiest way to make trading profits would be for the entrant either to take significant short or long positions in the incumbent's stock, or to trade options written on the incumbent's stock. Concerning the latter, there seem to be no impediments to taking large option positions on another firm, so long as options are currently traded for that firm. The only possible impediment would be a qualitative one: for instance, as the entrant tried to buy more and more put options on the incumbent, the price of these puts would likely increase. This would only serve to attenuate the possible gains from trading profits, however.

Concerning short positions in the incumbent's stock, there are some practical and institutional features that merit consideration. First, there are exchange-based rules that require any short sale to occur only on an "uptick," that is, when the price of the shorted stock increases. This generally imposes problems for short selling only when the stock is in a prolonged decline, but this is not a significant difficulty for the practice that I am examining. A more binding difficulty is that the volume of short selling, while appreciable, is frequently not large enough to allow the accumulation of large short positions in any one stock. For example, in late 1989 the top 1 percent of firms in terms of the percent of their stock sold short had on average short positions equal to 13.5 percent of their outstanding shares, and the top 5 percent of firms had short positions averaging only 6.1 percent of their outstanding shares (IDSI Quarterly Data). There have been recent cases, however, where firms have had over 25 percent of their stock sold short (Govoni 1990, 41). If the data were available, a more useful analysis would look at the percent of outstanding shares sold short by a single individual or firm, but the existing data at least show that large short positions do indeed occur.

Interestingly, short selling benefits from not being constrained by laws similar to those that hamper acquiring large long positions in a company. One important difference is the rule (the Williams Act) that requires investors to disclose whenever they acquire 5 percent or more of a company's stock. The large number of companies and the congressional hearings that have called for a similar disclosure rule when an individual's short position in a company exceeds 5 percent suggest again that large short positions in one company by a single entity are not only feasible but do frequently occur (Salwen 1991, C1).

For both financial and legal/ethical reasons, the trading strategy proposed here may appear risky. On the financial side, however, the profits from a short position in the incumbent's stock might be more certain than the profits from entry itself: after all, entry might not end up being profitable for the entrant, but entry will definitely hurt the incumbent.

On the legal/ethical side, it is possible that even if existing laws do not prohibit the activity, rational firms may choose not to engage in this trading strategy simply because of litigation fears or fears of negative publicity. I suspect that any company engaging in this proposed trading strategy would not advertise that fact. On the other hand, analysts of pension funds have suggested to me that it would be reasonable to expect a company's pension fund management to use its information on the entire industry in structuring its portfolio. Such behavior could be expected if the portfolio manager knew anything at all about his company's activities.[23] (It would not be unusual for a corporate officer—say, the vice president of finance—to oversee the pension fund, ensuring an information flow from the business side to the investment side.) Indeed, if a pension fund manager were privy to his company's activities, it is difficult to see how he could fail to use that information in his own portfolio decisions without violating his fiduciary duties. Suppose, for example, that Polaroid had been executing a stock offering just when Kodak made its discovery of an instant film process: when Polaroid's investment bankers called on the Kodak pension fund manager, would we expect that manager to be an eager buyer of the new Polaroid securities (assuming that the Kodak fund manager knew of Kodak's discovery)? Indeed, this higher expected return could be a good reason for a company to manage its own pension fund rather than have true outsiders perform that function.

IV. Entry and Entry Deterrence Models

A. Entry with a Passive Incumbent

Let's begin by showing how trading profits alter the standard entry economics with a passive incumbent. To keep the analysis simple, assume that there is one incumbent firm already set up to serve a one-period market and that there is one potential entrant that would incur a fixed, nonrecoverable entry cost if it entered the market. This fixed cost is known privately by the entrant and is believed by others to be a random draw from a probability distribution. As I proceed, I will refer to three types of profit: the profit earned by the entrant upon entry (which unless otherwise stated will be the profit before subtracting fixed cost), the profit earned by the incumbent if entry occurs, and the profit earned by the incumbent if no entry occurs (monopoly).[24]

Imagine that the profit earned by the entrant upon entry and the profit earned by the incumbent if entry occurs are determined through a competitive process whenever entry does occur (I will not model that competitive process). Similarly, profit earned by the incumbent if no entry occurs (monopoly), is determined through the incumbent's decisions on pricing and output as a monopolist. Assume that the profit earned by the incumbent when no entry occurs is greater than the incumbent's profit with entry, and that all three parameters are known to all parties (which means that demand and marginal costs must be known).

With these assumptions, a discussion of the decision to enter the market is easy; figure 5.1 illustrates the situation. If the potential entrant's fixed cost is less than the profits by the entrant upon entry, entry yields a net profit and will be undertaken. The probability of entry is thus a function of these uncertain fixed costs.

Now introduce the possibility of cross-trading by the entrant (this presumes publicly traded securities for the incumbent),[25] where the entrant can take either a long or short position in the incumbent's securities. A short position will be combined with the decision to enter and a long position with the decision to not enter. Profit from either of these trading strategies depends on two factors: first, how much the incumbent's market value changes with the entrant's decision; and second, how much of any value change can be captured by the entrant.[26]

In this example, there exists a critical fixed entry cost below which entry will occur if and only if the entrant's gross profit exceeds that fixed entry cost. This critical cost level must now be consistent with rational expectations, for the incumbent's market value before the entry announcement will both depend upon and determine the criti-

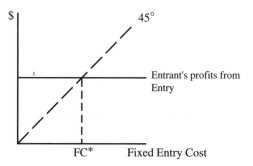

Figure 5.1 Entry without cross-trading: where FC* is the critical value of fixed entry costs below which entry will occur

cal cost level. In brief, an equilibrium value for this critical fixed cost will be such that the implied market value for the incumbent must be consistent with the entrant using FC* as the critical cost level.

Cross-trading profits from changes in the incumbent's market value alter the potential entrants returns to entry. The market value of the incumbent before knowing the challenger's decision to enter will be its expected monopoly profits resulting from no entry plus the incumbent's expected competitive profits if entry does take place. If the entrant enters, the profit it can make from short selling the incumbent's stock equals the percentage of the incumbent's value change capturable by the entrant through a short position times the change in the incumbent's market value. However, if the entrant can credibly commit not to enter the market, he can profit from holding a long position because the precommitment market price for the incumbent's stock is depressed by the possibility that the incumbent will lose his monopoly rents. Thus, if the entrant commits not to enter, his profit from holding the incumbent's stock equals the percentage change in the incumbent's stock value captured by the entrant times the change in the incumbent's market value.

With cross-trading of stock, the "full" net profit from entry before subtracting fixed cost but after recognizing the opportunity cost of not entering and taking profits from the resulting increase in value of the incumbent equals the entrant's profit from entry plus his profits from a short position minus profits that could have been obtained from a long position.

Figure 5.2 illustrates the equilibrium. The profit from short selling is decreasing with the critical fixed entry cost since as it increases, the value change of the incumbent upon entry decreases. Similarly, the profit from taking a long position in an incumbent's stock is increasing with respect to this critical fixed entry cost; the end result is that the "full" net profit from entry is decreasing with respect to this critical fixed entry cost. At FC_e^*, the incumbent is valued properly, given the decision rule optimally followed by the entrant: enter if and only if its fixed cost is less than FC_e^*.

Cross-trading stock thus makes it even more difficult to infer whether entry is encouraged or discouraged. If entrants are able to capture the same share of either an increase or decrease in the incumbent's value, the simple answer is that it depends. Figure 5.2 is drawn so that $FC_e^* > FC'$ where FC' is the critical cost level in the no-cross-trading case; allowing cross-trading in this case promotes

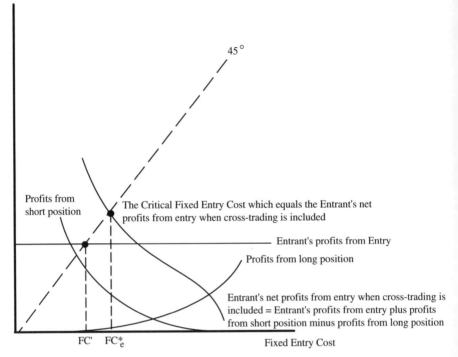

Figure 5.2 Entry with cross-trading: FC′ represents the critical value of fixed costs below which entry will occur if there is no cross-trading and FCe* the critical value if cross-trading is allowed (curves represent the statements that are closest to them)

more entry. This will clearly result whenever the possible short position profits are greater than the possible long position profits at FC′. But if the entrant is able to capture the same percentage changes in the incumbent's value through large short and long positions, it is straightforward to show that the gains from short selling will exceed the gains from going long if and only if the probability of entry with that fixed cost is less than 50 percent. Intuitively, short position profits exceed long position profits when the probability of entry is low, so that entry comes as a "surprise," and vice versa. The following proposition summarizes cross-trading's effect.

Proposition 1. If short and long positions offer equal profits to the entrant (for the same change in incumbent value), then the possibility of cross-trading has a "leveling" effect on the probability of entry: if the probability of entry is less than 50 percent without cross-trading, it will be higher with cross-trading, and vice versa. (Appendix C provides a formal proof for this.)

The analysis to this point suggests additional straightforward implications. Most important, note that anything which reduces the long position profits relative to the short position profits will result in a greater equilibrium probability of entry. This result is important because there are several reasons why long position profits may be more difficult to obtain than short position profits. First, several current laws make long positions more costly to achieve or limit the profits available from long positions. The Williams Act requires disclosure when any individual acquires 5 percent or more of any one company; such disclosure will necessarily signal that somebody is acquiring a large interest in the company and will likely cause the share price to rise, thereby limiting further profits. Antitrust laws of course also restrict the ability of any one company to take a long position in competitors' stock.[27] In contrast, there are no legal restrictions on short positions, and it is not clear that acquiring a large short position is any more costly than a similarly sized long position.[28]

Second, commitments to enter are more credible than those not to enter. A firm announcing its entry into a new market typically accompanies the announcement with details of products, distribution, etc., and will thus likely be believed (and thus incumbent firms' share prices will react strongly). In contrast, a firm announcing that it will *not* enter a new market might find it difficult to signal its commitment not to enter. For example, suppose the potential entrant produced generic drugs and had been working on developing a substitute for some branded drug. Such a firm would be unlikely to dismiss all of its R&D staff just because it decided to not produce the one specific drug. Therefore it could easily revoke its earlier decision and continue to pursue the new market. In such circumstances, the incumbent firm's share price will react relatively little to the "no-entry" decision.

B. Entry with an Entry-Deterring Incumbent

In this section I will expand beyond the viability of any single entry deterrence scheme. My goal is to show how entry deterrence is affected by the possibility of trading profits, and entry deterrence is therefore modeled with a somewhat unspecified "entry deterrence technology."[29] For simplicity, the incumbent is allowed to invest in a bond that serves to signal his intent to maintain a certain output level in the face of entry. Given the presence of such a bond and the resulting commitment, an entrant must expect lower profits upon entry than if, say, a Cournot-Nash equilibrium held. In the absence of trading profits, the bond therefore serves to *reduce* the critical fixed cost level and therefore *reduces* the probability of entry. Of course, the incumbent will choose to set up the bond only if its benefits from deterring entry exceed the costs of setting up and maintaining the bond.

If entrants can take trading profits, the economics of entry deterrence change. By committing itself to a relatively large output upon entry, the incumbent lowers profits for itself as well as for any other potential entrant. The predatory incumbent's stock price falls far more from entry than if it had not committed to the larger output. This, however, also increases the trading profits that an entrant stands to gain from a short position.[30] Thus, the entry deterrence strategy can end up backfiring, by giving the entrant short position profits in return for the incumbent's losses. Predation may actually cause firms who had never contemplated entering the market to enter now. But, on the other hand, the incumbent's strategy also implies greater trading profits to a potential entrant who does not enter and has taken a long position in the incumbent's stock: the news of no entry will be more favorable to the incumbent's stock price because it means that the lower profits from the high output post-entry will be avoided.

The results from relying on the more general ability to deter entry differ somewhat from those found in the preceding discussion, which focused on a single entrant. Suppose that without cross-trading the optimum probability of entry chosen by the incumbent is less than or equal to 50 percent. This is the case where short selling increases the return of entrants to entering the market. With cross-trading, the marginal benefit of increasing the incumbent's entry-deterring bond *must fall*. Short selling motivates the incumbent to lower the bond, and therefore the probability of entry will increase. This is similar to the outcome seen previously in section IV(A). However, if, in the absence of cross-trading, the profit-maximizing probability of entry is greater than 50 percent, cross-trading might increase or decrease the marginal benefit of increasing the bond and therefore increase or decrease the optimum probability of entry. The crucial difference arises because a potential entrant's decision to commit not to enter has a smaller effect on the incumbent's stock value simply because other entrants still have the option of entering. The reason for the ambiguity is that while in the preceding section raising the probability above 50 percent would have increased the return to going long and committing not to enter, as the probability rises above 50 percent the return to an individual entrant making a commitment is also smaller because it becomes more likely that another potential entrant will enter. (This discussion is proved more formally in Appendix C.)

V. Summary and Extensions

Secondary financial effects can be important for firms' behavior. The secondary effects should be incorporated into economic models. Hirshleifer's (1971) seminal insight regarding inventors taking trading profits from the price adjustments resulting from their innovations can be applied much more broadly. Indeed, the possible extensions of his analysis go beyond predation theory. A long list of such potential trading profits can easily be pointed to: output decisions of publicly traded oligopolists; new product introductions; auctions and bidding (if bidding to buy something, bid lower than the Nash equilibrium bid,[31] but supplement this bid with a long position in other bidders); and advertising campaigns. Virtually any action a firm undertakes seems likely to impact its competitors and thus could be analyzed in terms of this discussion of trading profits.

Trading profits tend to have a leveling effect on the probability of entry—increasing the likelihood of entry when the probability without trading profits is low and decreasing the probability when it would otherwise be high. For example, the more successfully a predator deters entry, the greater the return that trading profits create toward producing new entry. Creating a reputation to predate can thus be self-defeating. This chapter indicates that there is a possibility that trading profits will more likely encourage entry and competition than prevent them.

The analysis might help explain existing insider trading laws and the asymmetric treatment of investors disclosing long and short positions. For disclosure of position rules, the chapter points out that recent efforts in Congress and the Securities and Exchange Commission to make the Williams Act symmetric and create a reverse 13D rule can involve unforeseen costs. Mandatory disclosure of short positions will reduce the profit potential from a variety of competitive actions—entry into another company's market foremost among these—and therefore reduce the likelihood of these actions. For insider trading, if trading on material nonpublic information is indeed harmful—for instance, if it causes bid/ask spreads to widen—, it would seem that there should be no distinction between trading in one's own shares or trading in one's competitor's shares. Yet, I have shown that rules which allow trades where one company takes a position in another on the basis of material and nonpublic information have redeeming efficiency aspects because they can encourage entry into markets.

This focus on trading profits could also prove useful in reanalyzing many important limit pricing and predation cases. For example, U.S. Steel is one of the classic cases of limit pricing (Parsons and Ray 1975 and Stigler 1965): it was accused of charging a supracompetitive price for steel but kept the price low enough to discourage new entry. Note that U.S. Steel was publicly traded, something very important in the analysis here. Short positions in U.S. Steel by potential competitors would reduce the effectiveness of limit pricing, while long positions would accomplish the reverse. The American Tobacco Company was publicly traded at the same time it was accused of numerous predatory pricing events between 1891 and 1906 (e.g., Burns 1986). Trading profits may also require us to reexamine some classic cartel situations. Even the famous Trans-Missouri U.S. Supreme Court case (1897) involved railroads that were publicly traded concerns (Binder 1988). In terms of my discussion, the relevant question is the returns that fellow cartel members would obtain by going short in the other cartel member's stocks and then breaking the cartel agreement. Of course, long positions work in the opposite direction and reduce the returns to reneging on agreements.

The cross-trading of stocks raises an issue only briefly discussed in this book: diversification. Robert Hansen and I (1996) showed that shareholders do not want value maximization if shareholders own diversified portfolios and if companies impose externalities on one another. Instead, shareholders want companies to maximize the shareholders' portfolio values, and this occurs only when firms internalize between firm externalities. Hansen and I discussed a wide array of pecuniary and nonpecuniary externalities involving both vertical and horizontal relations between firms, but we ignored predation, which involves an extremely large externality that a firm can produce. Yet, our evidence indicated that diversified stock ownership internalized many of the externalities that firms imposed on each other. For example, not only were we able to explain the prices that firms paid during mergers based upon the degree of cross-ownership between the merging firms, but there was evidence of firms' internalizing the costs of patent and R&D races. In another interesting example, Albert J. Wilson, vice president and secretary of TIAA-CREF, claimed that the large pension fund had been instrumental in applying pressure to ensure that the Pennzoil v. Texaco and Apple v. Microsoft conflicts were resolved, and he asserted that this pressure caused Pennzoil and Texaco to settle their suit much sooner than they would otherwise have done.

While none of the above cases dealt directly with predation, it is interesting to see how diversified portfolios have caused many different types of externalities to be internalized. However, two thoughts should be mentioned. First, this argument provides another reason why nontraded private firms might be relatively more likely to engage in predation (though private ownership does not ensure that the owners are not to some extent diversified). Evidence of how stock ownership causes firms to internalize their externalities can be seen in the prices paid for acquired firms in mergers. The evidence indicates that the price firms pay in mergers is positively related to the degree of stock cross-ownership between the acquiring and the acquired firm (Hansen and Lott 1996, 59–65). Nontraded private firms—where such cross-ownership is small—internalize the smallest share of a higher bid, and paid the smallest premium when they acquired publicly traded firms.

Second, diversified ownership might more likely lead to cartelization than to predation. However, this too might not be a very serious problem, but here again diversified stock ownership can help internalize the deadweight loss from monopoly. If the firm maximizes its value and has monopoly power in the product market, it will choose an output where marginal revenue equals marginal cost; marginal cost will therefore be less than price, which equals the marginal value of the firm's output to consumers. Any shareholder who consumes some of the product would like a higher output: the last unit's marginal profit contribution is zero but its contribution to consumer utility is positive. In the "perfect" case, where each customer holds the same number of shares and has the same demand curve for the product (and therefore consumes the same quantity), and where there are no nonshareholder consumers, there will be unanimity over how the firm should operate: produce the competitive output, i.e., where price equals marginal cost.[32]

Finally, this chapter's discussion on short selling an incumbent's stock also provides a link with my earlier discussions on the relative return to predatory behavior by government enterprises. The ability of privately held concerns to escape having their stock shorted by potential entrants of course also applies to government enterprises, since government agencies have no stock that can be sold short.

SIX

Some Final Thoughts

Predation may exist, but the courts have been at a loss in knowing what to look for, and in recent years economists have provided very little useful guidance. The last two decades have seen a multitude of game-theoretic models of predation trying to sort out the issues. But the models are diverse and offer a virtually uncountable number of different scenarios. Many view this as a virtue: "After learning the basic facts about an industry, the analyst with a working understanding of oligopoly theory should be able to use these tools to identify the main strategic aspects present in that industry" (Shapiro 1989, 408–409). Others have gone so far as to advocate abolishing economists' traditional notion of individual rationality because doing so would allow us to produce many more models (Stiglitz 1992). With no more than anecdotal evidence and a couple of empirical tests that are incapable of even differentiating predation from perfect competition, many economists have forcefully argued that it is "unfortunate" that the courts have not relied more upon game-theoretic models (see, e.g., Klevorick 1993, 166). Not only does it seem incumbent upon economists to argue persuasively that these models apply to the "real world," but it is unclear what we expect the courts to do when multiple explanations exist for a single observation.

Fortunately, the courts in this country still require a higher standard of proof than does the economics profession. Yet, without being able to provide the courts with some notion of which of the myriad models to pick or how to provide ways of testing whether these theories are empirically important, industrial organization risks irrelevancy. Anecdotal evidence and case studies will not be sufficient. *119*

Economists have claimed to provide systematic evidence, only to then be forced to rely on vague court testimony to differentiate whether their tests imply predation or competitive behavior. Even when such evidence exists, interoffice memos between executives discussing "beating" or "demolishing" a competitor may not mean the same thing to those executives as some economists read them to mean.

My goal has been to provide systematic empirical evidence that can differentiate predatory from competitive behavior and can test whether game-theory models actually predict observed firm behavior. The models of predation that I have examined included reputational models with and without well-defined last periods as well as so-called signaling or long purse models.

This book has examined whether the assumptions underlying several predation models hold up under empirical scrutiny. I have tested whether managerial preferences can prevent last period problems that arise during predation. I have also tested the more recent reputational models where there are no last periods. There was no evidence that firms accused or convicted of predation obtained a greater return to entrenching their managers; instead, these firms were actually more likely to link managerial salaries to short-term profits. Such a linkage between salaries and profits makes it very costly for a manager to sell output below cost as required by predation. The manager would reduce his salary while the firm was making investments in a predatory reputation, but—without entrenchment—managers risk not being around when the return to the predation begins to pay off. None of the existing models of predation is consistent with the observed pattern of managerial compensation.

My evidence in fact helps justify the courts' general skepticism regarding predation. However, not all the courts in the country share this attitude. The Ninth Circuit Court of Appeals has rendered particularly perverse decisions, in that the court punished firms for predation that did the opposite of what the predation theories predicted. Possibly, this is not too surprising given the Ninth Circuit's peculiar definition of predation based simply upon one firm harming another, but it does raise some concern about the risks involved in letting courts determine whether predation has occurred. Even if the law is attempting to solve a real problem, the law does not necessarily produce the desired end result.

My analysis has also allowed us to evaluate some recent policy debates on restricting the use of short selling. To the extent that predation is considered a real threat, short selling represents one method of ensuring that new entrants are able to profit from their knowledge of whether they will enter a particular market.

In two chapters I have argued that government enterprises are more likely than private firms to meet the assumptions of these game-theoretic models. The belief that private firms are profit maximizers is so widely held that the assumption that all potential competitors believe otherwise is difficult to accept. If the notion of nonprofit objectives is at home anywhere, one would think that it is most at home within the government. After we control for numerous possible political biases against government firms in nonmarket economies, the results show that governments themselves appear to view government enterprises as more of a predatory threat than they do private enterprises. Yet, despite the vast involvement of government enterprises in even the American economy—from education to health care to transportation to postal services—, all different types of countries subscribe to the self-serving notion that it is only government enterprises from *other* countries that create inefficiencies.

Few people (economists especially) would argue that public universities are inherently superior to private universities (in terms of either cost or output). Yet because of below-cost pricing, there has been a continual rise in the share of students attending public universities.[1]

As demonstrated in this book, predations by government and private enterprises have one important feature in common: they represent a joint hypothesis test involving these theories of predation and whether the legal system can properly identify and punish those who are actually violating the law. Possibly both sets of results fail for the same reason: that the government does not accurately punish those who have violated the law. However, if that is really the case, it provides scant comfort for those who advocate an aggressive government policy to deal with predation. Why should we place our trust in a government to implement a policy which it is failing to enforce properly?

Possibly this failure of antitrust policy is not too surprising. George Stigler (1985, 7) wrote that support for "the Sherman Act came from small business interests" who desired protection from more efficient competitors. These small firms may have justified the law as protection against predation, but, from a wealth-maximizing point of view,

Stigler's evidence indicates that the motivation for this law was no different than that for high tariffs barriers. Indeed in 1890 the strongest supporters of the Sherman Act, including Sherman himself, were supporters of high tariffs to protect their constituents from competition (Hazlett 1984). The broader question asked by this book is should the government pick which firms will be allowed to succeed? In cases like Microsoft, do we feel better having the government and the courts pick what technologies we will be choosing among? The evidence in this book is consistent with Stigler's and Hazlett's hypothesis that antitrust enforcement was intended to punish more efficient firms rather than to increase efficiency.

So where should future research be headed? I believe that one fruitful avenue would be to investigate collusion in the same way that this book has examined predation. The theories of collusion have thus far not been scrutinized this way, and it would be useful to provide a competitive explanation of observed pricing behavior as an alternative hypothesis. Then the evidence could be used to distinguish between the two. The current practice of providing evidence that is consistent with a theory is a long way from providing evidence that proves the theory.[2] This approach has mistakenly led economists to believe that predation is more frequent than it actually is.

Explaining the Framework Used to Evaluate the Legitimacy of Anti-dumping Cases

The General Agreement on Tariffs and Trade (GATT) establishes a framework under which importing countries investigate alleged dumping by foreign producers. The anti-dumping laws seek to prevent anti-competitive pricing that is not directly motivated by government industrial or trade policy. Because firms in nonmarket economies are government-owned, the line is blurred between subsidized exports and below-cost exports. A possible objection to focusing upon anti-dumping charges, therefore, is that some "subsidy" cases may be brought as "dumping" actions in the case of nonmarket firms, thereby biasing my data set. This bias does not appear very plausible. First, subsidies are treated legally as distinct from predatory behavior for both market and nonmarket firms. Anti-competitive pricing resulting directly from government production or export subsidies is instead regulated under the countervailing duty laws. Countervailing duty cases have in fact been brought against firms in nonmarket economies (see Finger and Olechowski 1987, 260–263).

Second, even if the dumping cases in my sample had included those instances where nonmarket firms charged low prices as a result of receiving government subsidies, a strong argument can be made that those cases should be included in my measure of dumping. There is no analytical distinction between a parent company providing a subsidy to one of its subsidiaries which then engages in predatory behavior and incurs losses, and a government subsidizing its enterprise for the purpose of engaging in below-cost pricing.

Dumping complaints are most typically raised by import-competing firms. These firms are required to demonstrate "sufficient evidence" of dumping before the domestic government will initiate an investigation.[1] Anti-dumping investigations involve extensive inquiries into the foreign firms' pricing practices and their effects on domestic firms' economic health. If dumping charges against an exporting firm ultimately are substantiated, the importing country may impose an offsetting duty. A successful anti-dumping complaint must prove both that the imports have been sold for less than their normal value and that they have materially injured domestic competitors. Traditionally, the "material injury" test has been interpreted extremely leniently. A reduction in domestic employment, output, or profits associated with increased imports from the offending country is typically considered to satisfy the material injury requirement. For this reason, in most anti-dumping investigations attention centers on the "below normal value" pricing requirement. After taking into account differences between the two countries in the circumstances of sale and the products' physical characteristics, if the good's export price is less than its "normal value," this latter requirement is deemed to be satisfied.

The GATT requires member countries to measure a good's "normal value" by its customary price in the exporter's domestic market whenever this price is regarded as providing a "reliable free market" benchmark (GATT, Art. VI, para. 1). In practice, the domestic price in the exporting country is deemed reliable if there exists a moderate volume of sales of the product involving arm's-length transactions. This price discrimination definition of dumping is the most frequently applied in investigations involving exports from market economies. The GATT specifically notes that domestic prices in nonmarket economies are unlikely to provide a meaningful normal value benchmark for comparing export prices (GATT, Ad. Art. VI, para. 1, Sec. 2). Therefore, in nonmarket economies, where sufficient arm's-length sales do not exist, the GATT offers two alternative definitions of normal value: (1) the price charged by the exporting firm in a third country, and (2) the good's cost of production in the exporting country plus allowances for selling costs and profit.

The choice of which alternative definition to apply rests with the investigating country. Because the price charged by a nonmarket exporter in third countries is likely to be regarded as unreliable whenever that firm's domestic price is rejected, most countries have adopted the cost-based definition of normal value for nonmarket economy exports. Thus, Australia, Canada, the European Economic Community (EEC), and the United States consider "sales below [the] fully allocated cost of production ... [that] have been made over an extended period of time and [that] do not permit recovery of all costs within a reasonable period of time" to satisfy the pricing below normal value test (Jackson and Vermulst 1989, 444). This concept of fully allocated cost in international trade law corresponds to economists' understanding of long-run average cost.

The United States estimates nonmarket exporters' long-run costs of production using a constructed-cost methodology. Investigators first identify the amounts of each input that the nonmarket enterprise uses in the good's production, and then value these at "free market prices" taken from a third country at the same level of economic development as the actual supplier (Jackson 1989b, 295–296).[2] The estimated total cost of production is then simply the sum of these components, plus an allowance for selling costs and profit. Australia, Canada, the EEC, and Finland employ a slightly modified constructed cost methodology, using the surrogate country's factor proportions as well as its input prices in their calculations.[3]

This constructed cost methodology could potentially bias upward the estimation of nonmarket firms' costs of production.[4] A country will export those goods in which it has a comparative advantage. The third country whose costs are used to construct the estimate of the nonmarket firm's costs may not have the same comparative advantage in that product. In this case, using the factor costs from the third country will produce an upwardly biased estimate of the nonmarket economy's true production costs, increasing the likelihood of an incorrect affirmative dumping decision.

The method of determining costs for firms in market economies could also produce an upward bias. For example, the accounting rules used to derive the good's cost of production in the exporting economy are based on historical and not actual replacement costs. Thus, even if no dumping were actually occurring, it could still be in domestic producers' interest to bring dumping charges against foreign exporters whose historical costs of assets were high relative to the current market cost of replacing them. In such cases, foreign exporters' price could lie below their accounting costs, even if price exceeded true economic costs. Dick (1991) provides empirical evidence that incorrect measurement of firms' costs in the presence of learning-by-doing was apparently responsible for successful anti-dumping investigations against Japanese semiconductor producers.

Data Appendix

The 59 countries in my sample of anti-dumping complaints are: Argentina, Australia, Austria, Belgium-Luxembourg, Brazil, Bulgaria, Canada, Chile, China, Colombia, Costa Rica, Czechoslovakia, Denmark, Dominican Republic, East Germany, Ecuador, Egypt, El Salvador, Finland, France, Greece, Hong Kong, Hungary, Iceland, India, Iran, Israel, Italy, Japan, Kenya, Malaysia, Mexico, Netherlands, New Zealand, North Korea, Norway, Peru, Philippines, Poland, Portugal, Qatar, Republic of Korea, Romania, Singapore, South Africa, Spain, Surinam, Sweden, Switzerland, Thailand, Trinidad & Tobago, Turkey, United Kingdom, United States, USSR, Venezuela, West Germany, Yugoslavia, and Zimbabwe.

Analyzing How the Profitability of Entry Deterrence Is Affected by the Possibility of Trading Profits

The discussion in the text can be stated more formally, where:

π_{EE}:   Profit earned by the entrant upon entry, before subtracting FC

π_{IE}:   Profit earned by the incumbent if entry occurs

π_{IM}:   Profit earned by the incumbent if no entry occurs (monopoly)

M_0:   Incumbent's market value before the challenger's decision to enter

π_L: Entrant's profit from holding a long position in the incumbent's stock and then not entering the market

π_S: Entrant's profit from short in the incumbent's stock and then entering the market

F(FC): Probability distribution of the fixed entry cost (FC)

The incumbent's market value before the challenger's decision to enter equals:

$$M_0 = F(FC^*) \, \pi_{IE} + (1 - F(FC^*))\pi_{IM} \qquad (A1)$$

The profits from shorting or going long in the incumbent's stock are given by:

$$\pi_S(FC^*) = 1_S(M_0 - \pi_{IE}) \qquad (A2)$$

and

$$\pi_L(FC^*) = 1_L(\pi_{IE} - M_0) \qquad (A3)$$

where FC* is the critical cost level that the market assumes the entrant to be using and the dependence of π_S and π_L on FC* (through M_0) is explicitly noted, and $\pi_S(FC') - \pi_L(FC') > 0$.

To more formally analyze entry deterrence, I model the incumbent as being capable of putting up a "reputational" bond that signifies his commitment to maintain a certain output level in the face of entry. If the bond amount is B, then the cost of this bond is cB per period; c can be interpreted as the cost of setting up and maintaining a reputation. With each bond amount B, there is associated a quantity $q_I(B)$ which is the quantity that the incumbent commits himself to produce upon entry. If the incumbent does indeed live up to this commitment, he receives his bond back at the end of the period (less cB). If the incumbent does not produce $q_I(B)$ upon entry, he forfeits the entire bond.

Notice that $q_I(B)$ will generally be different from the Nash-Cournot output for the incumbent with one entrant. If I let $\pi_{ID}(q_I)$ represent the entry-deterring incumbent's profit margin with the output of q_I, it will then be true that

$$\pi_{ID}(q_{ID}) \leq \pi_{IE} \tag{A4}$$

where π_{IE} is the incumbent's profit margin with one entrant and the Nash-Cournot output. Furthermore, π_{ID} will be decreasing in q_I, and this in turn means that the difference $(\pi_{IE} - gp_{IE}(q_I))$ will be increasing in q_I. But $(\pi_{IE} - \pi_{ID})$ determines whether or not the incumbent will forfeit his bond upon entry; if $B < (\pi_{IE} - \pi_{ID})$ the incumbent is better off forfeiting the bond and producing the Nash-Cournot output. It follows that the equation

$$B = \pi_{IE} - \pi_{ID}(q_I) \tag{A5}$$

implicitly determines q_I as a function of the bond size, and that q_I is increasing in B: to commit to a higher output takes a larger bond.

The key question for the entry-deterring incumbent is how his commitment will affect entrants' decisions. If an entrant cannot take trading profits, then it will enter iff $FC < FC^*$, where FC^* is defined in

$$FC^* = \pi_{EE}(q_{ID}) \tag{A6}$$

with $\pi_{EE}(q_{ID})$ being the entrant's business profits from entry when the incumbent produces q_{ID} post-entry.

If trading profits are available to entrants, then the equilibrium is determined in

$$FC_e^* = \pi_{EE}(q_{ID}) + \pi_S(q_{ID}, FC_e^*) - \pi_L(q_{ID}, FC_e^*) \tag{A7}$$

As before, π_S and π_L depend upon the current expectations for FC*, the critical cut-off level of fixed cost, because that determines the incumbent's *ex ante* market value. With entry deterrence, π_S and π_L also depend upon q_{ID}, for that determines how much "damage" entry will do to the incumbent.

It is crucial to note that by choosing a bond amount and therefore q_{ID}, the incumbent chooses the level of FC* (in (9)) or FC_e^* (in (A7)). As I elaborate below, this will be done by balancing the benefits of a higher q_{ID} against the costs. The question of interest is, of course, the impact that cross-trading has on the selection of q_{ID}. The following proposition gives the answer.

Proposition 2. Let FC' be the critical cost level determined by an entry-deterring incumbent without cross-trading. If F(FC') < ½, then the critical cost level chosen with cross-trading will be greater than FC'. If F(FC') > ½, then in general it is impossible to say whether cross-trading leads to a higher or lower critical cost level.

On the surface, Proposition 2 looks like Proposition 1 in the text where the effect of cross-trading on entry deterrence depends on whether the *ex ante* probability of entry is less than or greater than ½. There is an important difference, however, that can be highlighted by briefly reviewing the analysis behind Proposition 2.

In determining an optimal level of entry deterrence—the optimal bond size—the incumbent will compare the costs of posting a larger bond against the benefits. The benefit of a greater q_{ID} is that it reduces FC_e^* (reduces the probability of entry). Differentiating (A7) with respect to q_{ID} yields:

$$\frac{\partial FC_e^*}{\partial q_{ID}} = \frac{\partial \pi_{EE}}{\partial q_{ID}} + \frac{\partial \pi_S}{\partial q_{ID}} + \frac{\partial \pi_S}{\partial FC_e^*}\frac{\partial FC_e^*}{\partial q_{ID}} - \frac{\partial \pi_L}{\partial q_{ID}} - \frac{\partial \pi_L}{\partial FC_e^*}\frac{\partial FC_e^*}{\partial q_{ID}} \quad \text{(A8)}$$

Rewriting, I get

$$\frac{\partial FC_e^*}{\partial q_{ID}} = \frac{\dfrac{\partial \pi_{EE}}{\partial q_{ID}} + \left[\dfrac{\partial \pi_S}{\partial q_{ID}} - \dfrac{\partial \pi_L}{\partial q_{ID}}\right]}{1 - \dfrac{\partial \pi_S}{\partial FC_e^*} + \dfrac{\partial \pi_L}{\partial FC_e^*}} \quad \text{(A9)}$$

which describes the marginal benefit to the incumbent of increasing the post-entry output it commits to. In the case of no cross-trading, I would have

$$\frac{\partial FC_e^*}{\partial q_{ID}} = \frac{\partial \pi_{EE}}{\partial q_{ID}} \tag{A10}$$

Equation (A9) differs from (A10) in two ways: first, (A9) has a denominator on the right-hand size; and second, there is an additional term in the numerator, which is itself a difference between two derivatives.

Looking at the denominator of (A9) first, one can see that it exceeds 1: $\partial \pi_s/\partial FC_e^* < 0$ and $\partial \pi_L/\partial FC_e^* > 0$. *Thus, the impact of having this denominator in (A9) is to make $\partial FC_e^*/\partial q_{ID}$ smaller than it otherwise would be* (which is the case of no cross-trading). This effect can be seen in figure 5.2 by noting that the impact on FC_e^* for a decrease in $(\pi_{EE} + \pi_S - \pi_L)$ is less than for the same vertical decrease in π_{EE}. The reason for $(\pi_{EE} + \pi_S - \pi_L)$ having a negative slope is of course that $\partial \pi_s/\partial FC_e^* < 0$ and $\partial \pi_L/\partial FC_e^* > 0$.

The numerator of (A9) however makes the effect of cross-trading on entry deterrence somewhat ambiguous. Just as the difference between π_S and π_L depends on the probability of entry occurring, so does the difference between $\partial \pi_s/\partial FC_e^*$ and $\partial \pi_L/\partial FC_e^*$. I can say for sure that if $F(FC_e^*) \leq 1/2$, then

$$\frac{\partial \pi_S}{\partial q_{ID}} - \frac{\partial \pi_L}{\partial q_{ID}} > 0 \tag{A11}$$

and therefore $\partial FC_e^*/\partial q_{ID}$ is smaller in absolute value than otherwise. If $F(FC_e^*) > 1/2$, then the inequality in (A11) might hold but need not; so it is not possible to say anything about the overall impact on $\partial FC_e^*/\partial q_{ID}$.

Chapter One

1. The most prominent early proponents of this view are Milgrom and Roberts (1982b) and Kreps and Wilson (1982). For a general survey of this literature see Rasmusen 1989. Rasmusen (1988) discusses how retaliatory threats against potential entrants can sometimes backfire. See also chapter 2.

2. I am not suggesting that all assumptions of game-theoretic models should be taken literally. Rather, if *key* assumptions of these models were unrealistic, it would be difficult to argue that the models apply to real world situations.

3. Results from the general idea of one firm's trading in another's securities have implications for antitrust policy, insider trading rules, the Williams Act, short selling rules, corporate pension fund management, whether companies should be publicly or privately held, and the degree of diversification for companies.

4. Because of these difficulties Carlton and Perloff limit government policy to the extreme "where the effects of the strategic behavior is unambiguously harmful." Many game-theoretical economists would not concede that these cut-and-dried cases ever exist, and would argue that one can only get a feel over time for whether undesirable strategic behavior was motivating a firm's behavior.

Gates, Milgrom, and Roberts (1995) argue that, while predation by the Regional Bell Operating Companies was a theoretical possibility, on the basis of theoretical arguments such predation was "highly unlikely." They make this claim because government regulations of prices eliminate the ability to charge monopoly prices after predation occurs. This argument is undoubtedly true, but it is not clear what insight game theory adds to this point.

5. Others have a different view of what it means "to be able to test something." For example, Stiglitz (1992, 138) writes, "advances in sociology and psychology . . . have shown that there may be systematic patterns to individual behavior, even when they are irrational . . . the fact that behavior is not rational, in some sense, does not mean that it is not predictable." Stiglitz goes on to argue that seeming empirical regularities can take the place of testable hypotheses. If the results then change over time, we must supposedly presume that people are acting in some new irrational manner. Stiglitz also has a different view of what I would regard as the foundations of economics and at the same time provides what I regard as a concern over the perceived use of game theory. He writes (p. 138) that "one of the central contributions of game theory has been to make it clear that the 'rational' actor model is not only inaccurate . . . , but internally *131*

incomplete and/or inconsistent ... Game theorists have increasingly relied in their analyses on 'small' degrees of irrationality, while at the same time showing that the exact nature of the equilibrium depends precisely on the nature of these small irrationalities ..." Incidentally, did we really need game theory to tell us that if people behave strangely it will affect the equilibrium?

6. As an example of the difficulties involved in interpreting anecdotal statements, one can look at Weiman and Levin's reference to Southern Bell Telephone's rejection of offers from a Lynchburg, Virginia, competitor to raise rates and refrain from taking each other's customers (p. 114). Weiman and Levin write, "Perceiving that its [Southern Bell Telephone's] plant was in better condition than its competitor's, [Southern Bell Telephone] preferred to fight a war of attrition." Obviously, however, showing the possibility that Southern Bell Telephone had lower costs than its independent competitor is not the same thing as proving predation. Nor is evidence that Southern Bell Telephone may have initially lost money while it charged low prices to build up a customer base. The value of a Southern Bell Telephone telephone to customers is in part dependent on the number of customers using their telephones. Charging lower prices to begin with can be viewed as an investment in customer services, like a telephone company laying the cables to handle the telephone traffic. It is costly to acquire customers, but doing so increases the amount that customers are willing to pay in the future. The question of whether this is competitive behavior depends upon whether these costs and benefits are being equated at the margin.

Incidentally, there is not enough information given in their fn. 21 to determine whether Southern Bell Telephone had lower costs than the independent company. For example, in the extreme, if all the customers for both companies were residential users, the costs for Southern Bell Telephone would have been $5,352, while the costs would have been $4,730 for the independent company. The rankings would be reversed if all the customers were business customers.

7. In another frequently discussed paper, Bresnahan (1987) attempts to explain the 4 percent drop in automobile prices and the 38 percent increase in "auto quantity" between 1954 and 1955 along with the subsequent 2 percent rise in automobile prices and the 16.5 percent decrease in "auto quantity" between 1955 and 1956 as resulting from a temporary breakdown in the collusive arrangement between automobile manufactures. (As an aside, I view these numbers as reflecting a remarkably elastic industry demand curve for a monopolistic industry.) The empirical evidence Bresnahan provides relies upon structural supply and demand equations where, in the presence of market power, the supply equation includes a term for the demand elasticity. Yet, even in a competitive world, it is not clear why changes in demand do not affect the type of product being produced by these car companies and thus in turn could affect the costs of production. (See Demsetz 1982a for a discussion on the difficulties inherent in measuring the marginal cost of production.)

Bresnahan also offers no monopoly-type explanation why General Motors should be the company selling the most underpriced cars. With its dominant share, General Motors instead ought to be the company to obtain the largest monopoly rents. A competitive explanation why General Motors had the largest market share was simply that they were able to charge low prices because they were more efficient. Bresnahan claims that this could be due to General Motors cars having a quality advantage, but it seems more likely that it could arise because General Motors cars were at a quality disadvantage and thus could not command the premium paid for the car of other makers.

8. Some information on the overall importance of oil shipments to railroad profitability would also have been useful in this discussion. Presumably, one could argue that the lost profits on the monopoly oil shipping charges to non-Standard Oil companies were small relative to the benefits obtained from enforcing railroad cartel agreements for the shipping of other products. However, Granitz and Klein's discussion is in terms of a "cartel in petroleum transportation" (p. 2).

9. *Eastman Kodak Co. v. Image Tech. Servs., Inc.,* 112 S. Ct. 2072 (1992).

10. Jonathan Baker (1994, 43) claims that the court did not pass judgment on what he terms the post-Chicago game-theoretic views of predation in the Brown & Williamson case, and thus he argues that the court may indeed be sympathetic to these game-theoretic views. "These post-Chicago developments were not noted by the Court in Brooke Group, and they were not brought to the Court's attention by the parties to the case. In sharp contrast, briefs before the Court in the Kodak litigation referenced and discussed the post-Chicago economic literature relevant to that case. Against this background, it is not surprising that the Court relied exclusively on Chicago School ideas concerning price predation and oligopolistic coordination in Brooke Group, while accepting a post-Chicago economic perspective concerning the issues addressed in Kodak."

11. For a discussion of the American Airlines case and the federal jury's decision to acquit, see Ellen Neuborne, "Lawsuit Could Curb Price Wars," *USA Today,* August 25, 1993, 4B. Continental and Northwest Airlines sought more than $3 billion in damages from American Airlines. They alleged that a price war that American instigated in 1992, where they reduced coach fares by an average of 38 percent and eliminated most discounts, was an attempt to drive them out of business.

Not everyone was satisfied with this decision. Alfred Kahn has argued, "The way big airlines respond to competition from start-ups could objectively be described as predation." Richard Tomkins, "When Fares Aren't Fair," *Financial Times* (London), February 10, 1998, 21.

12. While we will discuss the Microsoft case in depth later, recent discussions by both the U.S. Departments of Transportation and Justice have focused on predatory practices of the four largest airlines. Indeed the government points to concerns that "Five small carriers have vanished in the past nine months, and only one new carrier has gotten aloft in the past 18 months." In order to stop these alleged problems, the Department of Transportation "intends to scrutinize use of frequent-flier awards and travel-agent bonuses for possible anticompetitive effects." Bruce Ingersoll, "Air Carriers Face 'Dumping' Enforcement," *Wall Street Journal,* March 13, 1998, 3 and 6.

13. *Brooke Group Ltd. v. Brown & Williamson Tobacco Corp.*, 113 S. Ct. 2578 (1993). The Brown & Williamson case is also the first Supreme Court decision on predatory pricing under the Robinson-Patman Act since the Utah Pie case in 1967 (*Utah Pie Co. v. Continental Baking Co.*, 386 U.S. 685 (1967).

14. Some have argued that this 12 percent market share is misleading because Brown & Williamson's branded sales were disproportionately reduced by Liggett's sales of generic cigarettes (Burnett 1994, 271). Indeed, there is some evidence that Brown & Williamson suffered about 20 percent of the total drop in branded sales. Yet, even if this is true, it still leaves a very large free-rider problem, and it is difficult to explain why Brown & Williamson was the firm that engaged in the predation.

15. Given the ease of moving production from the branded to generic markets, it is particularly difficult to believe that predation in such a narrow segment of a market could be successful.

16. *Matsushita Elec. Indus. Co. v. Zenith Radio Corp.*, 475 U.S. 574, 588–593 (1986) and see also *Cargill, Inc. v. Monfort of Colorado, Inc.*, 479 U.S. 104, 121 n.17 (1986) for a similar discussion.

17. *Brooke Group Ltd. v. Brown & Williamson Tobacco Corp.*, 113 S. Ct. at 2588 (1993). See for example, Boudreaux et al. 1995, 57, for a similar discussion.

18. Glazer (1994, 46) writes: "No elaborate analysis is required to recognize that, with Brooke Group, predatory pricing suffered a great setback. What is less obvious is that this setback may have been fatal to all future predatory pricing claims. Liggett's evidence was so unusually strong that plaintiffs will be unable to persuade already hostile courts that their case is worthier than Liggett's of reaching a jury. This may sound counterintuitive given that the market share of the defendant in Brooke Group was only 12 percent and that therefore the case is easily distinguishable. As will be demonstrated, however, plaintiffs suing defendants with much higher market shares, even dominant-firm level market shares, will be hard pressed to match the quality of Liggett's evidence regarding the anticompetitive character of the industry involved, the defendant's own analysis of its and the plaintiff's role in that industry, and the defendant's pricing behavior."

While the court evidently sent a strong signal, it could have gone even further than it did. For example, the Supreme Court could have created a rule of per se legality to govern price cutting by members of noncollusive oligopolies. Instead it noted that "however unlikely that possibility [of noncollusive oligopoly predation] may be as a general matter, when the realities of the market and the record facts indicate that it has occurred and was likely to have succeeded, theory will not stand in the way of liability": *Brooke Group Ltd. v. Brown & Williamson Tobacco Corp.*, 113 S. Ct. at 2591 (1993).

19. See Boudreaux et al. 1995, 58, for a detailed discussion of the Utah Pie case.

20. With newspaper headlines reading "Predatory Business Practices" or "Microsoft's Chief Concedes Hardball Tactics," it is difficult to rule out a predation case being brought against Microsoft. (See John Hall, "Predatory Business

Practices," Scripps Howard Newspapers Wire Service, March 5, 1998, and John R. Wilke and David Bank, "Microsoft's Chief Concedes Hardball Tactics," *Wall Street Journal* ,March 4, 1998, B1.)

21. Christy Hudgins-Bonafield, "Will NT Server Bail under Vendor Pressure?," *Network Computing*, January 15, 1998, 30.

22. Fortunately for Microsoft the antitrust standards used in the Alcoa case (*U.S. v. Aluminum Co. of America et al.,* 148 F. 2nd 416 (1945)) are no longer applicable. In that case Alcoa was punished because its superior skill, foresight, and industry had allowed it to outcompete its rivals. As Judge Learned Hand wrote (pp. 430–431):

> The successful competitor having been urged to compete, must not be turned upon when he wins . . . [However] It was not inevitable that it should always anticipate increases in the demand for ingot and be prepared to supply them. Nothing compelled it to keep doubling and redoubling its capacity before others entered the field. It insists that it never excluded competitors; but we can think of no more effective exclusion than progressively to embrace each new opportunity as it opened, and to face every newcomer with new capacity already geared into a great organization, having the advantage of experience, trade connections and elite personnel.

There were no allegations that Alcoa charged prices below cost and no denying that customers had benefited from Alcoa's hard work, but, despite Judge Hand's words to the contrary, the very fact that it had competed so hard that it won the market was used against it.

23. Still others might be concerned about issues like "raising rivals' costs." In this case, some have pointed to the large hiring campaigns that Microsoft has engaged in where they have hired many key employees of companies like Apple who were working on projects that competed with Microsoft. See Salop and Scheffman 1987.

24. The desire to apply this notion of inefficient lock-ins has gotten completely out of hand. For example, Douglass North (1991) goes so far as to claim that he can explain the adoption of different government policies using this argument. Yet, it is not clear why there is a similar free-riding problem with government institutions. If all voters would be made better off by switching government institutions, they would simply pass legislation that required the form of government to change. It is not a question of a few voters attempting to change government institutions without the consent of other voters.

25. Objections to what Microsoft bundles in with the operating system also have a certain arbitrariness. Many features of Windows 95 or 98 could obviously be sold separately from the operating system, just as car companies could sell cars without radios or even engines. However, at least for cars, the normal presumption is that the benefits that customers obtain from this additional choice is small compared to the costs that they would face in combining cars with different engines after the rest of the car has already been built.

26. Dvorak's study is so farcical that it is amazing that it has been given any

weight by economists (Leibowitz and Margolis 1990, 10–12). Those trained to use the Dvorak and QWERTY keyboards had quite different previous training and abilities. For example, those trained to use the Dvorak keyboard appear to have already been competent typists, while several of those who were trained on the QWERTY keyboard initially scored zero on their typing tests. Later tests by the Navy in 1956 were unable to find any advantages from the Dvorak keyboard.

27. Hilton's book describes in great detail the careful engineering studies that went into the choice of gauges that railroads finally agreed upon.

28. It appears that the VHS format originally accepted a larger and hence less convenient cassette size because of its longer recording time (Leibowitz and Margolis 1995a). In terms of technical performance, the two formats were comparable, in part because of cross-licensing agreements between the companies. Even though Beta had a head start, occupying the entire market for several years, VHS surpassed Beta soon after its introduction, as customers apparently preferred a longer recording time to a smaller package. There is no evidence that BETA was superior in any dimension that mattered to customers.

29. See Leibowitz and Margolis 1995b for an excellent discussion of the assumptions behind these concerns about lock-ins.

30. See Bork 1978, 365–381, for an excellent discussion on tying arrangements.

31. Paula Rooney, "Netscape Navigates Retail Concerns after Free Browser Download Offer," *Computer Retail Week,* February 9, 1998.

32. As a final example, the Clinton administration's Department of Transportation wants new regulations of airline service and pricing practices to stop what it call actions that are "analogous to (and may amount to) predation." The department's proposed policy contained a classic statement of predation where:

> Before the new entrant does withdraw, the major carrier, with its higher cost structure, will carry more low-fare passengers than the new entrant, thereby incurring substantial self-diversion of revenues— i.e., it will provide unrestricted low-fare service to passengers who would otherwise be willing to pay higher fares for service without restrictions. Consumers, for their part, enjoy unprecedented benefits in the short term. After the new entrant's withdrawal, however, the major carrier drops the added capacity and raises its fares at least to their original level. By accepting substantial self-diversion in the short run, the major prevents the new entrant from establishing itself as a competitor in a potentially large array of markets. Consumers thus lose the benefits of this competition indefinitely. (Requests for Comments on Department of Transportation Enforcement Policy Regarding Unfair Pricing, Department of Transportation, Office of the Secretary, [Docket No. OST-98-3713])

Chapter Two

1. Rasmusen (1989) provides a general survey. Rasmusen (1988) also discusses how retaliatory threats against potential entrants can sometimes backfire.

2. Jensen and Murphy (1990) are frequently cited as showing that managers get very little of the profits from wealth maximization and that they are not likely to be dismissed unless profits are very low. If true, the question is whether there is an implicit divorcement of management from ownership and whether one should thus expect to find no differences between predatory and nonpredatory firms. More recent evidence examined by Khanna and Poulsen (1995) indicates substantially higher annual managerial turnover rates than those suggested by Jensen and Murphy, above 30 percent among financially distressed firms (twice the rate they found for firms making average returns), and implies even greater expected financial losses to managers from dismissal (see also Boschen and Smith 1995). However, even if one accepts Jensen and Murphy's lower estimates indicating that manager replacement rates range from 11 percent for firms earning the market rate of return during the two preceding years to 17.5 percent for firms earning 50 percent less than that rate for two years (p. 239), it is hard to ignore the importance of entrenchment in motivating managers. Earning the average market return for 3.15 years (the average length of the alleged predatory behavior I will show in the sample) implies a 24 percent probability of dismissal, while earning 50 percent less than the average for 3.15 years raises the probability to 38 percent, a 58 percent higher turnover rate than the average. Lower earnings are something one expects during predatory periods. Jensen and Murphy's (p. 241) estimates of the expected wealth loss 45-year-old managers face from dismissal equals up to $3.5 million in lost salary if they manage a firm earning 50 percent less than the market return for 3.15 years. Their estimates imply that including lost compensation from stock ownership can easily quadruple the total expected wealth loss.

3. For discussions of models which examine the role of nonvalue-maximizing agents see Milgrom and Roberts 1982b and Lott 1990 and 1995.

4. Klein (1984) provides a discussion of hold-up problems in labor markets. For a discussion of hold-up problems in a variety of settings see Klein et al. 1978.

5. As Milgrom and Roberts (1982b) note, it is the difficulties posed by facing a limited time horizon or less than an infinite number of potential competitors that motivated them to begin with. Their paper was an attempt to solve the unraveling problem.

6. Karpoff and Malatesta's results confirmed earlier findings by DeAngelo and Rice (1983) and Linn and McConnell (1983) that antitakeover charter amendments were motivated by a similar desire to protect incumbent management. Meulbroek et al. (1990) and Malatesta and Walking (1988) provide additional evidence that antitakeover charter amendments entrench management.

7. Likewise, larger firms should be more difficult to buy, because the greater borrowing required to take over larger firms creates incentives for managers to make riskier decisions, which should raise borrowing costs (Jensen and Meckling 1976).

8. Knoeber (1986) also suggests that research intensity makes it more difficult to remove management because of the need to protect managers from being held up for their sunk investments made in developing projects.

9. Following this logic, sole proprietorships and closely held firms should be the easiest vehicles with which to undertake predatory strategies because these firms do not suffer from the agency problems of separation of ownership and control.

10. Important problems exist with using Tobin's q and make us question the usefulness of this measure. Since Tobin's q relies on the book value of firms, it often tells us more about accounting artifacts (e.g., the age of an industry's assets) than about how well industries have done over time. Demsetz (1982a) provides a general criticism of the claim that different profit rates can exist in an industry when all assets are priced at current market values. When assets are priced in terms of their true opportunity costs, concepts like Tobin's q are rendered meaningless. Any variations in values then are a result of mistakes in properly valuing a firm's assets.

11. Consistent with this prediction, Morck, Shleifer, and Vishny (1989) found that the average target of a hostile takeover had a lower industry-adjusted Tobin's q ratio than other firms.

12. Rasmusen (1991) surveys earlier signaling models, among the most prominent examples being Milgrom and Roberts 1982a and Roberts 1986. His paper improves upon these earlier models by dropping the unrealistic assumption that potential entrants are unaware of their costs.

13. One problem with the long purse is that there is a market for undervalued assets, so that there is an incentive to take over credit-constrained firms.

14. See also related papers by Klein (1996), Lott (1988 and 1996), and Shapiro (1983).

15. Liebeler writes (p. 1052) that to his knowledge predatory pricing charges arose in "approximately fifty-five cases in the federal courts." The additional case noted above is a result of the inclusion of Austin's sample, which included a slightly longer time period. I used the cases identified by Liebeler and Austin to ensure a consistent method of identifying all the predation cases that occurred within this time period. If I had expanded the sample past 1988, cases like *Brooke Group Ltd. v. Brown & Williamson* (61 U.S.L.W. 4699 (1993)) could have been included. However, this case shows how difficult it has been to bring predation cases after the Supreme Court's 1986 Matsushita decision. In fact, in this case, the Supreme Court said that even if Brown & Williamson had attempted predatory pricing, there was inadequate evidence to show "it had a reasonable prospect of recovering its losses from below-cost pricing."

16. The AT&T case with MCI (708 F.2d 1081 (7th Cir. 1983)) was the only observation which I lost because of the additional constraint of using the COMPUSTAT.

17. The initial search was performed on Lexis using the search command "predatory pricing and date aft 1957 and date bef 1992" in the "genfed" library and "dist" sublibrary. There were 277 citations that contained the phrase "predatory pricing" in the district court sublibrary. A majority of these cases had nothing to do with predation. A commonly found example of an irrelevant reference to predation is the citation of a previous case that involved predation, but was

cited in the current case for other, nonpredation, reasons. Some individual predation cases accounted for several of the 277 citations. A single case, for example, would have three or four citations due to various procedural motions throughout the district court level.

18. I thank Tom Harris for supplying data on chief executive officers' turnover rates and on management compensation.

19. Controlling for this does not alter my results.

20. Jonathan Karpoff kindly provided these data.

21. Related to the question of the endogeneity of lawsuits, the theory of predatory pricing offered by Milgrom and Roberts and others assumes that entrants cannot sue. Interestingly, while plaintiffs won 6 out of the 21 appeals court cases, plaintiffs won only one of the 47 additional district court cases. Defendants appealed all but one of the cases that they lost at the district court level and a possible reason for not appealing the one case was the relatively small size of the total monetary penalty ($115,000). The expected rate at which plaintiffs win these suits appears to be about 10 percent (7 divided by 68). The true rate could be either higher or lower since, as noted in the text, the cases where firms were the most obviously guilty were presumably settled out of court, and it is unlikely that legal action was threatened in all cases were predation occurred.

22. Besides the accused and convicted dummy variables, I also tried controlling for firm size (as measured by the log of total assets, sales, and employment) and year and industry dummies or simply the year and industry dummies and obtained similar results. Removal of the Ninth Circuit Court of Appeals cases leaves the signs of the coefficients unchanged but reduces their level of significance.

23. One possible objection is whether I am studying managerial incentives at the appropriate level of the firm's hierarchy. While data are available only for CEO compensation, the pricing and production decisions are probably made by divisional or geographic managers. This seems especially plausible for some of those firms in the sample that deal with multiple products. Yet, I assume that the ultimate responsibility resides in the CEO, and the shareholders must provide appropriate incentives for the CEO to hire "aggressive" lower-level managers. If predatory behavior by lower-level managers reduces the CEO's compensation, the question is why a CEO would encourage those actions.

24. Firms with the same 4-digit SIC code were ranked by market share using TRINET data. The firms closest in size to the firm accused of predation were then chosen for inclusion in table 2.4. The TRINET database provides information on over 700,000 establishments (i.e., plants, administrative offices, or other separate geographic business locations) that employ 20 or more persons in United States. TRINET classifies each establishment according to a primary 4-digit SIC code and provides information on the establishment's number of employees and its estimated sales in current dollars.

25. The results are not sensitive to whether I use the log of sales and assets in the regressions.

26. One possible explanation for this result is that there is a nonlinear re-

lationship between compensation and sales and that as sales are increased, the reward to managers increases at a progressively slower rate. However, adding a squared term for sales and interacting it by PREDATION YEAr does not alter my results.

27. The precise relationship is:

$$\mathcal{E}_{dPredator} = \mathcal{E}_{dMarket} - ((1 - Predator's\ Market\ Share)\mathcal{E}_{sNonpredator\ firms}).$$

where the predator's elasticity of demand, $\mathcal{E}dPredator$, must be greater than 1 if changes in the predator's sales are to be positively correlated with changes in the predator's output.

28. Assumptions concerning how rivals react to predatory actions are not central to my results since I am comparing predatory firms to all other firms in these regressions. In addition, while I generally assume that rivals react by "rolling over" and not by "fighting back" and expanding output, four of the rivals' supply elasticities reported in table 2.5 are negative and thus imply that these results still hold even if "victim" firms fight back against predation. This case corresponds to the regressions described above where I reestimated the specifications after deleting the 13 cases where industry elasticities were less than 1.

29. Tobin's q is equal to the market value of equity plus the book values of debt and preferred stock all divided by the book value of a firm's assets adjusted for inflation by the producer price index. See note 10 for a related discussion.

30. Industry dummies are another method of controlling for these differences, but, unfortunately, the large number of dummies involved (whether I employed 2- or 4-digit SIC codes) prevented the logit estimates from converging.

31. As predicted earlier, firms which entrench their management may reincorporate in other states with takeover laws. I found no firms in the sample which reincorporated between the time in which they were alleged to have engaged in predation and 1991.

32. An equivalent OLS coefficient would be slightly less than two thirds as large as the logit coefficient on ownership concentration (see Maddala 1983, 23).

33. Unfortunately, the data provided by DeAngelo and Rice (1983) on antitakeover charter amendments do not identify the date on which those amendments were adopted. If the data had contained this information, it would have been possible to match the dates when those amendments were adopted with those when the predatory behavior is said to have occurred.

34. This allows us to deal with the question of endogeneity.

35. I ran this without including age and tenure since those are variables directly controlled by the firm, and if they wanted to, they could choose managers so that they had the desired ages and tenure when it became time to engage in predation.

Chapter Three

1. This discussion is related to questions on the general growth of government. Bennett and Johnson (1980) provide a useful survey of the arguments why

government has grown over time. Lott and Fremling (1989) explain the growth of government based upon the costs of voters evaluating the long-term versus short-term effects of government regulation. Kenny and Lott (1996) attempt to explain the growth in government as a result of giving women the right to vote.

2. Ellig (1989a) provides an interesting list of other similar cases.

3. The other solution to Selten's chain-store paradox is to assume that there is some probability that no last period will arise. I will deal with the plausibility of predation in the framework provided by Milgrom and Roberts. For a critique of the Bain-type entry barriers used by Milgrom and Roberts to limit the number of potential entrants, see Demsetz 1982a and b.

4. Borcherding (1971) has argued the reverse of output maximization and noted that public enterprises may actually act as monopsonists in cases where they face upward-sloping supply curves. Lott (1987c, 491–493), however, provides empirical evidence why that hypothesis can be rejected in the case of public schooling.

5. Alchian and Kessel (1962) provide evidence that public utilities divert some of their profit possibilities into nonpecuniary forms of income when accounting profits reach the limit set by state regulatory commissions. See Borcherding 1977 and Borcherding et al. 1982 for further evidence on the behavior of public bureaucracies.

6. Johnson and Libecap (1989b) provide some evidence that agency growth significantly increases the salaries of government workers, but the effect is very small. Wilson (1989, 180–181) argues that the evidence that bureaucrats desire to maximize agency output is weak, though he does mention that this is a quite widely held belief. Even if Wilson is correct, it does not affect my central argument, since he argues that people are more likely to believe that public enterprises have output-maximizing objectives than do private firms (p. 118).

7. Lindsay (1976, 1072–1073) finds empirical evidence that public enterprises produce more of those outputs that can be easily monitored by politicians (e.g., the number of patient days in a hospital) than will be produced by proprietary enterprises. (See Clark 1988 for some more recent evidence supporting Lindsay's hypothesis.)

However, James Q. Wilson (1989, 180–181) provides both anecdotal and systematic empirical evidence against the notion that government agencies are intent on maximizing size. In particular he (p. 180) points to findings that government agencies have "declined a chance to grow or actually approved of losing a subunit." He explains away the perception that government agencies have a predisposition toward growth as arising because "We hear more about the former [agencies attempting to expand] than the latter because expansionist agencies make more noise (often the noise of smaller agencies being gobbled up), whereas the latter go about their daily business quietly."

Jensen and Meckling (1976) discuss the response of principals to the anticipated shirking by agents.

8. In addition, as Demsetz (1982a, 54) notes, economists cannot even differentiate why predation by owners who value higher future profits is different from

by a private predatory firm's owners who intrinsically value harming their rivals or altruistic owners who like spending their wealth by giving a product to customers below cost.

9. Of course, as Niskanen (1975, 635) notes, this is the extreme case, and his model predicts that the most likely outcome is to observe both higher costs and higher output than the efficient output. The greater the extent to which a public organization maximizes its discretionary budget, the less is the threat posed to private profit-maximizing firms. (De Alessi [1980] and Clark [1988] provide extensive surveys of the relative costs of public and private enterprises.)

10. Obviously, if firm P is interested in maximizing its short-run output, the social loss will be larger. For instance, it can set price where the demand curve intersects the average variable cost curve.

11. In Lott 1987b, I argue that the threat of competition reduces an agency's rent extraction by an even larger amount than that suggested by Niskanen. (See also Niskanen 1974.)

12. There were 157 parks in the system at that time. This discussion predicts that if the National Park Service had been allowed to retain a larger portion of the fees, they would have increased entrance fees even further.

Libecap (1981, 75) also provides a discussion of the incentives of the Bureau of Land Management to raise fees for livestock grazing once certain political restrictions were lifted. Johnson (1985, 115–116) notes that after 1908 the U.S. Forest Service was able to retain only 10 percent of the receipts from timber, with 25 percent going to local counties and the remainder to the U.S. Treasury.

13. Using Niskanen's (1975, 620–621) model provides a simple example of the cost that a public enterprise's manager faces if he sets a single monopoly price (i.e., MR = MC). Niskanen assumes that the bureaucrat's utility function takes the form:

$$U = \alpha \, Q^\beta (TR - TC)^\gamma,$$

with total revenue and total cost given by: TR = P Q and TC = c Q + d Q^2, where P and Q are the prices and quantities that the public agency faces in selling its output. Assuming that the market demand curve equals P = a − b Q, the agency's total revenue function after the private competitor has been eliminated equals TR = a Q − b Q^2. Setting MR = MC implies a profit maximizing output of Q = (a − c) / [2(d+b)]. However, if the bureaucrat does not obtain any of the agency's profits (or "discretionary budget") in the form of income or perks (see Niskanen, p. 621 and the above discussion in the text), $\gamma = 0$ and the bureaucrat's ideal quantity is Q = (a − c) / (d+b), or twice the level of output of the profit-maximizing monopolist. Relaxing the non-negative profit constraint on the public enterprise or allowing price discrimination would of course result in even greater levels of output.

14. Explanations for tie-in-sales based upon price discrimination by private enterprises have also been widely discussed (e.g., Kenny and Klein 1983 and also Lott and Roberts 1991 for a discussion of the difficulties in identifying price discrimination). While the conditions for price discrimination's feasibility are the

same for both public output-maximizing and private profit-maximizing enterprises, the efficiency implications are quite different. While price discrimination for private firms can result in either an increase or a decrease in output, for public enterprises price discrimination will be undertaken only when it increases an already too large level of output.

15. For example, if there are limited resources and I wanted to maximize the number of students attending public school, higher quality public schools will have to be provided to wealthier families because they have more elastic demands for public schooling with respect to quality. There is some historical evidence that this was the case when public schools still charged fees for attendance (Lott 1987c). My discussion can easily be reformulated so that the bottom axis is in terms of quality units of the good rather than physical units.

The two-part pricing used by the federal government to price entrance for national parks (per car and per individual fees) can easily be interpreted in terms of price discrimination.

16. If I use the Niskanen-type explanation of why output maximization arises, the bureaucrats in this agency are made better off through price discrimination at the expense of the outside constituents who support the agency. Unlike what the Niskanen and Lindsay discussions conclude, however, the additional social losses from predation should also create additional opposition to the agency. The importance of this additional opposition from this new group of victimized firms depends upon such things as its costs of organizing and how dispersed the losses are. At the margin both effects will work to reduce the agency's support.

17. For a discussion on the role of a private predator acquiring the assets of the firms that were driven out of business see McGee 1958. He also provides strong evidence that even if such actions were in fact behind Standard Oil's acquisitions, it could not have been a successful strategy.

Chapter Four

1. For empirical tests of below-cost pricing among private enterprises, see Burns 1986, Elzinga 1970, Isaac and Smith 1985, Koller 1971, McGee 1958, 1980, and Yamey 1972.

2. See Appendix A for a more detailed discussions of these definitions of costs. See Posner 1992, 309, for a comparison between laws against predation and against dumping.

3. Chinese launches were estimated to have been 30 to 50 percent cheaper than those offered by American and European competitors. China was allowed to proceed with sales only after agreeing to provide launches at prices "on a par" with Western competitors and after agreeing to accept an annual quota of 1.5 launches through 1994 (Covault 1989, 37, and *Aviation Week & Space Technology,* December 5, 1988, 32). The Chinese defended their pricing strategy as investing in a reputation for dependability and argued that, in a broader definition of costs, their pricing did not constitute below-cost selling (see *Aviation Week & Space Technology,* September 19, 1988, 22).

4. Airbus is jointly owned by the British, French, and (West) German governments. The United States further charged that Airbus's pricing practices threatened to drive McDonnell Douglas out of the commercial aircraft market (Dunne (1990)).

5. Several legal observers have raised similar points. See, for example, the discussion in Palmeter 1989. None, however, has attempted to test whether such political biases can explain the distribution of anti-dumping cases or actions across countries.

6. Demsetz (1982a), Darby and Lott (1989, 94–97), and chapter 4 discuss some of the difficulties involved in determining whether below-cost pricing has occurred.

7. Davies and McGuiness (1982, 176–177) have noted that output maximization by private enterprises can lead to dumping because of a separation between ownership and control. My theory differs, however, by predicting that because government enterprises are more likely to value output (or revenue) maximization than their privately owned counterparts, they should constitute a greater threat to their competitors' profitability. Thus, dumping in my theory occurs as a result of a conscious decision process by the firm rather than from shirking. Davies and McGuiness (pp. 177–179) also note that the threat of dumping may convince a competitor not to enter the market. As I noted earlier, this constitutes a less credible threat on the part of private firms since while they may gain long-run benefits from increasing output, such behavior is very costly in the short run. Government enterprises, by contrast, not only receive long-term benefits from thwarting entry but also are made better off in the short run by expanding output. Finally, a small number of economists who study nonmarket economies have pointed out that firms from those countries appear to dump more frequently than do firms from market economies (Wilczynski (1966a and b, 1969)). However, to date, no systematic evidence has been offered.

8. A state-owned monopoly is likely to face a smaller entry threat from potential domestic competitors than will private firms in market economies in this situation. In practice, however, this advantage will be small whenever significant foreign competition exists. Given the wide availability of alternative sources of supply for the products most often involved in anti-dumping investigations (see Appendix A), state monopolies would not appear to offer an advantage over and above that stemming from the monopoly's ownership form.

9. As another example, an output-maximizing firm subject to a zero profit constraint can, by engaging in price discrimination, increase output by using the revenues from the higher priced inframarginal sales to subsidize below-average cost production at the margin. However, the higher prices will induce new entry, which will in turn lower output because of both lost sales and reduced rents. Both restrict the ability to subsidize below-cost production. With sufficient entry, an output-maximizing enterprise will even find it desirable to set price equal to average cost so as to increase output.

10. Both private and public enterprises may alter their pricing in different ways after driving competitors from the market (chapter 4 discusses this point). Just as it is not always necessary for a firm to be successful in driving competitors

from the market to be charged with predatory pricing under the antitrust laws, successful international dumping cases do not require that the exporter completely eliminate injured domestic firms. For theoretical discussions of predatory behavior see Bork 1978 and Demsetz 1982a.

While Areeda and Turner (1975) define predation as occurring whenever price is below average variable cost in the short run, GATT uses a long-run average cost criterion (discussed later in this section). These two measures are identical in the long run since all factors are then variable.

11. For example, in a case study of Australian dumping complaints between 1961 and 1966, Wilczynski (1969, 155–156) noted that the ratio of dumping complaints against nonmarket to market economies exceeded the ratio of Australia's volume of trade with these two types of economies. However, rather than seeking to explain his empirical observation or to study its extent and its causes, Wilczynski largely dismissed his findings as the product of incorrect measurements of nonmarket firms' production costs and political biases by Western governments against nonmarket economies (Wilczynski, 1966a, 257, and 1969, 161). Unfortunately, no evidence is offered to support either of his claims.

12. The classification of countries as nonmarket is based upon the 1988 Trade Act's requirements, and yields an identical breakdown to that in Gastil 1986 (15) and Finger and Olechowski (1987 (264–269)). The 1988 Trade Act codified the United States Department of Commerce's method of identifying nonmarket economies by using the following criteria: (1) the extent of government ownership or control of the means of production; (2) the extent of government control over the allocation of resources and the prices or output of the enterprises; (3) the extent to which the currency is freely convertible; (4) the extent to which wage rates are determined by bargaining between labor and management; (5) the extent to which foreign investment is permitted, including in joint venture form; and (6) other appropriate factors (Ehrenhaft, 1989, 309). While this chapter uses the GATT definition of market and nonmarket economies so as to be consistent with the rest of the discussion, I also tried another measure provided by Freedom House (Gastil 1986, 15) which used a somewhat more disaggregated breakdown of the level of government involvement in the economy. The results were qualitatively similar to the ones reported here.

13. Prusa (1989) notes that a significant fraction of anti-dumping charges initiated in the United States are withdrawn, either by the government or by the petitioning industry, before a final determination is reached. Prusa stresses the "threat" value of such cases and argues that they may be equally important in terms of their effects on the volume and pattern of trade as cases that are allowed to continue to completion. For this reason, in this chapter I attempt to explain the pattern of initiated anti-dumping cases as well as of affirmed cases.

14. Data for Finland were available only for 1983–1987.

15. Austria, Spain, and Sweden are included in the later empirical work in section IV(B), where I do not require the ability to identify the individual countries against which their complaints were brought.

16. An appendix which details how anti-dumping complaints are initiated and adjudicated is available from the author.

17. See Takacs 1981, Magee and Young 1987, and Salvatore 1989 for other recent empirical analyses of administered trade protection that adopt similar specifications. A related empirical literature, summarized well in Lavergne 1983 and Finger, Hall, and Nelson 1982, seeks to explain the interindustry pattern of tariff and administered protection. The data do not permit me to identify the industry involved in each anti-dumping investigation, thus precluding the inclusion of industry-specific variables in the regression specification. The very strong fits that I find for each estimation, together with the similar success reported for like models (see in particular Salvatore 1989), however, provide reason for confidence in the economic significance of these results.

18. I deflated the import and export series using, alternatively, a GDP deflator and import and export price deflators to aggregate the trade flow data across the sample years. The qualitative results were not sensitive to the choice of deflator, and therefore I report only the regressions using the export and import price deflators.

19. These data were available only for 1980–1985. However, their superior accuracy relative to other cross-country estimates of real GDP recommended their use. I calculated each country's average real GDP per capita for 1980–1985 and used this as the *REAL PERSONAL GDP*$_j$ variable in equation (1). Data for North Korea were taken from the CIA's *World Factbook* (1980–1985) and data for the Bahamas were taken from the United Nations' *National Accounts Statistics: Main Aggregates and Detailed Tables* (1986).

20. Real per capita GDP for the market economies in the sample was, on average, 18.3 percent higher than for nonmarket economies.

21. The Generalized System of Preferences established by the GATT is the most important and extensive set of tariff concessions granted by developed countries to less developed countries. Many developed countries have also granted other trade preferences individually. For a discussion, see Jackson 1989b, 278–281.

22. For a partial listing of nonfinancial government enterprises in different market and nonmarket economies, see International Monetary Fund 1987b.

23. Multicollinearity between export and import flows may also account for the inconsistent signing and often relatively low level of significance for these two variables.

24. The NONMARKET dummy in Canada's regression is significant at the 10 percent level for a single-tailed t-test.

25. For the linear regression on the initiated cases (column 1 in table 4.2), the bounds are: −0.229 to 0.0386 for IMPORTS AUSTRALIA, −0.0598 to 0.08165 for IMPORTS CANADA, −0.0105 to 0.00141 for IMPORTS EUROPEAN ECONOMIC COMMUNITY, −0.297 to 0.9247 for IMPORTS FINLAND, 0.00016 to 0.023 for IMPORTS UNITED STATES, −0.0181 to 0.019 for REAL PER CAPITA GDP, −20.064 to 88.075 for NONMARKET, −0.0495 to 0.3793 for EXPORTS AUSTRALIA, −0.1199 to 0.07498 for EXPORTS CANADA, −0.00216 to 0.01055 for EXPORTS EUROPEAN ECONOMIC COMMUNITY, −0.197 to 0.0322 for EXPORTS FINLAND, −0.0218 to −0.0000092 for EXPORTS UNITED STATES, and −95.97 to 128.99 for the intercept.

For the linear regression on the affirmative cases (column 3 in table 4.2), the bounds are: 0.0017 to 0.0207 for IMPORTS AUSTRALIA, −0.0162 to 0.0348 for IMPORTS CANADA, −0.00696 to 0.00176 for IMPORTS EUROPEAN ECONOMIC COMMUNITY, −0.01814 to 0.0062 for IMPORTS UNITED STATES, −0.0044 to 0.0113 for REAL PER CAPITA GDP, 3.3468 to 45.947 for NONMARKET, −0.04597 to 0.0081 for EXPORTS AUSTRALIA, −0.0453 to 0.0222 for EXPORTS CANADA, −0.0157 to 0.00658 for EXPORTS EURO-PEAN ECONOMIC COMMUNITY, −0.00516 to 0.0153 for EXPORTS UNITED STATES, and −62.3 to 22.3 for the intercept.

26. R_m^{*is} is defined by

$$R_m^{*2} = R^2 + (1 - R^2)\min_{ij}((1 - (B_{ij}/b_j))^{-1}).$$

B_{ij} is the jth coefficient from the ith normalized reverse regression and b_j is the jth coefficient from the direct regression (Leamer 1992).

27. I was also concerned about the possibility that the real per capita GNP variable was measured with more error in nonmarket countries than in market countries and that this might introduce systematic error in the results. To test if this measurement error could affect the results, I broke the sample into market and nonmarket groups and ran the direct and reverse regressions for the specifications shown in the first column of table 4.3 over each of these two groups of data. The concern was that the direct and reverse regression estimates would tend to be bounded for the market economies and not bounded for nonmarket economies. Because of the paucity of observations in the nonmarket economy case, I was unable to run these regressions for the specifications shown in table 4.2. In fact, I found no systematic relationship between the two sets of regressions. In the initiated cases, only for Canada did I find that the market economy estimates were bounded while the nonmarket economy estimates were not. The reverse was true for the United States, and for two countries the estimates for both market and nonmarket economies were bounded.

28. The existing literature has focused upon how factors such as industry employment, profitability, or political contributions affect the incidence of administered protection across industries (Finger, Hall, and Nelson 1982, Lavergne 1983). My interest here lies instead in how political forces may alter the relative incidence of anti-dumping charges between market and nonmarket exporters. While the same political influences that affect the interindustry composition of dumping complaints could in principle affect the distribution of market and non-market cases, the evidence reported in section IV(C) indicates that this is not the case. Thus, in contrast to the existing literature, my focus will be macroeconomic political forces rather than industry-level considerations.

29. For a discussion of disputes between the United States and Western European nations relating to the control of technology exports to the Eastern bloc, see Mastanduno 1988, 263–265. Olson and Zeckhauser (1966) discuss the free-riding problems associated with military expenditures.

30. Those countries most likely to be at war with the nonmarket countries should also have the greatest strategic incentive to protect their firms from the

negative effects of below-cost imports. Similarly, this higher probability of conflict may put government firms from nonmarket economies at a disadvantage in competing against Western private corporations because of the possible interruption of trade and cause them to charge lower prices in order to compensate buyers for relying on less dependable sources of production. As a result, these sellers will face a higher probability of being accused of dumping.

31. Unfortunately, data for affirmative decisions were not available in the same format. The data for Austria, Spain, and Sweden were not included in the earlier regressions because they recorded only whether charges were brought against the broad categories of market or nonmarket economies.

32. Alternative specifications which included the squared value of the country's nonmarket imports and exports and also removed the year dummies produced similar results.

33. The values of the t-test statistics for the null hypothesis that $\alpha 1 = \alpha 2$ were: 1.02 for specification 1, 0.73 for specification 2, and 1.29 for specification 3.

34. The value of the t-test statistic for the null hypothesis was 2.37.

35. Baldwin (1988), Finger, Hall, and Nelson (1982) and Ray (1981) provide extensive discussions of and evidence on the determinants of industries' success in lobbying for foreign trade protection.

36. Appendix A provides details on this discussion.

37. The anti-dumping and countervailing duty laws regulate "unfair trading practices." The regulation of "fair trade" that causes injury to domestic industries appears in Article XIX of the GATT, commonly known as the "escape clause." The escape clause is codified in United States law in Section 201 of the Trade Act of 1974. Section 201 makes no reference to below-cost (or discriminatory) pricing practices or to government subsidies. Because escape clause disputes do not deal with the issue of below-cost selling, I did not include them in the data set. It is worth noting in passing, however, that escape clause investigations treat all imports in an industry identically, regardless of the market organization form of the countries from which they are sourced. There exists a variant of the escape clause, Section 406 of the 1974 Trade Act, however, that applies only to exports from nonmarket economies when they lead to "market disruption." There have been approximately a dozen trade disputes brought under Section 406. Excluding from the data set these market disruption cases biases us against finding that nonmarket firms engage in dumping at a higher frequency than market firms.

38. Horlick (1989, 139) notes that as of the late 1980s nonmarket economies were precluded from being charged with countervailing duties. However, the data extends only until 1987 or 1986 depending upon the type of specification.

Chapter Five

1. There is no evidence that I can find of Kodak or Kodak-related individuals trading in Polaroid securities. However, during the period in which there was a lot of speculation over Kodak's entry, there was some peculiar trading in Polaroid's securities. For example, on November 28, 1973 (four months before Ko-

dak's official announcement), the Chicago Board of Trade restricted trading in certain Polaroid options. The reason given was to maintain an orderly market in the face of a buildup of uncovered short positions in the options (*Wall Street Journal,* November 29, 1973, 19).

2. In theory, Kodak could have written and sold call options before the announcement, and then bought those options back at lower prices on a subsequent day. However, since the issuance of such call options would be subject to the 1933 Securities Act's regulations, it seems impractical to exploit nonpublic information in this way.

3. As discussed in section III, the acceptance by many of the misappropriation theory implies that anyone other than the firm trading on this information may face insider trading charges.

4. More generally, a public firm may find that a large number of people are capable of determining the firm's business/financial situation through their dealings with it. Competitors, for example, will often know when a fellow competitor is doing very well or very poorly; suppliers, customers, and advisers will also often be in positions to gain what is, in essence, inside information. All these people could potentially trade in the firm's securities on the basis of their information. As established by Glosten and Harris (1988) and Glosten (1989), this creates adverse selection problems for the firm's securities dealers; they will in turn raise their bid/ask spread to protect themselves against losses. But a higher bid/ask spread implies higher transaction costs in this firm's stock; this means that the firm's cost of capital is higher, for the gross return on the stock must be high enough so that net returns—after transaction costs—are comparable to those of other securities. Thus, my general point is that public firms face a general disadvantage of a higher cost of capital to the extent that their business can be deduced by related parties (of course, this cost must be weighed against the benefits of being a public firm, for instance, being able to sell stock to a wide array of investors).

My discussion also provides yet another reason why government enterprises, which obviously do not have traded shares, have an advantage over publicly traded private firms in engaging in predatory actions.

5. I concede that this benefit to diversification was probably more important around the time of Jay Gould's business dealings than today. As I discuss in section II below, this may be true because in the late 1800s there were a number of large, monopolistic, single-business, publicly traded firms: railroads, steamship lines, and telegraphs, for example. This kind of business was especially prone to competitive entry, and the entrants sometimes found it easy to make trading profits in the incumbent's stock (see section III below for evidence). Diversification would have seemed to be an obvious response by the incumbent to partially close off at least one avenue of profit for entrants.

My argument on the benefits to diversification is more general than the entry story alone suggests. Again, a public firm may find that a large number of people trade in its securities using information that they derive from their business dealings with the firm. This "insider" trading raises bid/ask spread and therefore increases the cost of capital to the firm, so it would like to prevent it. One way to do so would be to diversify into several lines of business. If related parties gain information only on one line of the firm's business, then any position that they take in the firm's stock is necessarily more risky than if they could take a position in a security that represented just the one line of business they knew something about. Thus, the general argument for a benefit to diversification is that it makes it more difficult for related parties to take trading profits in the firm's stock; this may make the firm's business situation more secure (i.e., reduce profits to entry), and it should definitely lower the firm's cost of capital. A simple test of this theory would be to see if diversified firms do have lower bid/ask spreads than nondiversified firms.

6. See notes 4 and 5 on why insider trading might be costly: it raises transaction costs by increasing bid/ask spreads. Presumably, however, while those companies whose stocks values were hurt by insider trading by their own corporate officers would have an incentive to prevent it, it seems doubtful that similar steps exist for a firm to prevent such trading by other firms. (See also Manne 1966 for related discussions.)

7. It may be difficult to discover when firms short sell their competitor's stock simply because firms were not required to report publicly whenever they took these actions. Ironically, the *Wall Street Journal* article which provides the facts for my second case illustrates the difficulty involved in discovering these cases. The article discusses the event almost thirty years after it had occurred and was brought to the paper's notice by Mr. Park's associates. While it is clearly possible that the events discussed by the *Wall Street Journal* were publicly reported earlier, I was unable to find such an earlier reference.

8. The organizational structure of large companies (i.e., the fact that the people who have the relevant information differ from those who make the financing decisions) may also make it more costly for large corporations to exploit these informational advantages.

9. Some of the activities described by Gould may constitute illegal stock price manipulation today. For example, Grodinsky (276) claims that "Gould formed a stock pool in order to depress the price of Western Union." Likewise, my discussion in the next section describes a situation in which he was trying to force up the price of a stock. In both these examples, Gould seems to have been actively involved in spreading rumors about the future course of events.

10. As Grodinsky (277) writes, "the Western Union published its earnings and revealed the almost complete disappearance of the previous year's surplus of $1,600,000. This was followed by a dividend reduction . . . Reports and rumors spread thick and fast. 'A thousand rumors of the disastrous condition of the company, of the impossibility of its standing against the rivalry of the American Union, and of the implacable hostility of the latter, were skillfully circulated . . .'"

11. The line "What he might do to childish invaders exalted the spirits of every horror yearner" is very provocative. Does this allude to expected predatory actions on the part of Gould to force Park, the "childish invader," out of the market? What if Park's own company had been publicly traded—could

Gould have supplemented a strategy of predation with a short position in Park's stock? I leave these questions unaddressed for now.

12. Mr. Park is quoted by the *Wall Street Journal* as stating; "You ask what are my profits? I have made no profits. I have merely collected earnings—maybe a couple of millions. Earnings, not profits: if you doubt there's a difference, try toying sometime with that fellow Gould."

13. For his experience, Gould is quoted as saying, "Personally I stood some market loss— more, I figure, than an average season's wages for Mr. Trenor Park. But why worry? I own Panama Transit now. Really it was nice of him to start it for me. And I'm sorry I was snappy to him at that Pacific Mail meeting—say about $1,000,000 sorry."

14. There are even more ways that an entrant could take trading profits from its entry decision. Another prominent method is to take positions in firms downstream from the industry being entered, for these firms should increase in value with entry. The following excerpt illustrates yet another method that Jay Gould discovered:

> The eastbound livestock traffic soon emerged as the most conspicuous battleground. The usual rate from Buffalo to New York was $125 a carload. When [Commodore] Vanderbilt knocked the Central's rate down to $100, Gould put the Erie's at $75. The Commodore went to $50 only to have Gould drop to $25. Vanderbilt then decided to ruin the Erie's livestock traffic by setting his rate at the absurd figure of $1 per carload . . . Sure enough, the Central filled up with cattle while the Erie's cars ran empty. Vanderbilt cackled with glee until he discovered the reason for his easy victory. Unbeknown to him, Gould and [Jim] Fisk had bought every steer in Buffalo and shipped them into New York via the Central.
>
> "When the Old Commodore found out that he was carrying the cattle of his enemies at great cost to himself and great profits to Fisk & Gould, he very nearly lost his reason," [G. P.] Morosini laughed. "I am told the air was very blue in Vanderbiltdom." (Klein 1986, 97–98)

15. This is possibly not too surprising given that my historical examples sometimes did not come to light until decades after they had occurred.

16. This telephone conversation took place during August 1992.

17. Mr. Best informed me that unless I talked with the broker who took the order to make the short sales, it would normally not be possible to identify who was making the short sales, since he usually sees only the size and type of transaction being made and not who is making it.

18. Such trading could account for stock prices anticipating firms' earnings announcements by as much as 20 days. In the Dole case, the short selling should have put downward pressure on Dole's stock price prior to the announcement.

19. Another instance concerns alleged trading in government securities by Salomon Brothers, a large U.S. investment banking company. Henry Kaufman was an economist at Salomon Brothers who reputedly had the ability to affect securities prices significantly with announcement of his interest rate forecasts. It

has been alleged that Salomon Brothers would take securities positions to profit from Kaufman's announcements before they were made public ("A Debate on Ethics: Who Should Benefit by Kaufman's Ideas?" *Wall Street Journal,* August 19, 1982). While not exactly similar to the situation I focus on in this chapter, the case of Kaufman is similar in that a side benefit of Salomon's investment in Kaufman's expertise is the possible ability to make trading profits. This should have impacted decisions by Salomon Brothers on whether to engage in Kaufman's research, just as trading profits can impact decisions to enter a market.

20. For an up-to-date review of insider trading laws, see Barber 1987, Langevoart, 1986, Klein and Ramseyer 1994, and Wang 1996.

21. Carlton and Fischel (1983, 883–834) point out that this rule can apply differently to a firm's managers who make purchases based upon insider information. For example, they write (p. 884) "the purchase of a target's shares in advance of a takeover probably would be considered a usurpation of a corporate opportunity" to the extent that it raises the final price the firm must pay for the stock. In the context of chapter, those actions by managers would include short selling of a competitor's stock so that it reduced the gains to the firm from short selling that stock.

22. *United States v. James Herman O'Hagan,* 117 S. Ct. 2199 (1997). Prior to the Supreme Court's decision in O'Hagan, it was difficult to get a consistent reading from appeals courts on the acceptability of the misappropriation theory. The Second Circuit Appeals Court in Chestman defined misappropriation as occurring when "one who misappropriates nonpublic information in breach of a fiduciary duty and trades on that information to his own advantages violates Section 10(b) and Rule 10b-5." However, the court overturned Chestman's conviction because it was necessary that he understood that the information that he had been given resulted from a breach of trust and that the person who had told him that information also had a duty to withhold the information. Obviously, the misappropriation theory does not apply to one firm trading in another competitor's stock. As recently as the Carpenter case the Supreme Court had sidestepped the issue of misappropriation. (*Carpenter v. United States* 484 U.S. 19, 108 S. Ct. 316 and denied cert. in *United States v. Chestman* 947 R.2d 551 (2d Cir.1991) (in banc).)

23. For a formal model showing how an investor should use proprietary information to guide his security holdings, see Treynor and Black 1973. In their model, an investor will hold the market portfolio if he has no special information on any securities; if he has special information, then his portfolio can be thought of as a combination of the market portfolio and a portfolio of "bets," where the bets are in the stocks that he has special information on. The size of any bet depends upon the expected abnormal return on the respective stock and on the uncertainty (risk) associated with the return.

24. Similar concerns have been raised for other assumptions such as whether entrants can also have reputations (e.g., Carlton and Perloff 1990, 411), though the distinction discussed here over the type of information possessed by the entrant and incumbent seems even weaker. For the incumbent and entrant to have

similar reputations, it is necessary that the entrant already have business in other markets. For my discussion to work, it is only necessary that the entrant have better information than the incumbent on whether the entrant will decide to enter the market.

25. Throughout, I assume that the potential entrant makes a public announcement concerning its plans, and that this announcement is credible (as I discuss later, profiting through stock market trades that are based on misleading information constitutes fraud). In an efficient market, the value of the incumbent's securities will change immediately and completely upon the entrant's announcement.

26. The issue has arisen as to whether there are any investment actions that the incumbent could take to offset the entrant's cross-trading. If the entrant is a private company, this is a moot question. Even if the entrant is itself publicly traded, the incumbent lacks information on what the entrant will do and therefore has no means of deciding on a long or short position in the entrant. That is, the very nature of the situation makes the entrant the agent with private information and therefore the one who can profit from it. There might also be many potential entrants.

27. In fact, my discussion provides a possible efficiency explanation for the government's asymmetry in dealing with long and short positions. Long positions can reduce the incentive to enter an industry, while short positions will encourage entry. The 5 percent rule may thus reduce the size of long positions relative to short ones and thus reduce the returns to not entering a market.

28. Mechanisms exist which lower the costs of short selling. When a brokerage firm does not process sufficient shares to cover a short sale, it approaches custodian banks which will lend it the shares. Apparently there is no difficulty in acquiring shares, though these shares may have to be returned to the banks on relatively short notice. When a bank recalls its shares, one option is turn to other banks to replace them. In any case, the types of cases I am dealing with (such as the Dole Foods case) do not involve selling short a stock for long periods of time.

29. See Bernheim 1984 for related methodology.

30. Rational expectations with respect to the future losses a predator will be forced to incur if potential entrants can sell short the predator's stock implies that this will be incorporated in the value of the stock as soon as the commitment is made. However, even if the stock price fell when the commitment was first made, the price can still fall further when the entrant actually sells short the incumbent's stock and enters since there is uncertainty over whether the entrant's costs were sufficiently low to make entry profitable.

31. A Nash equilibrium is an array of strategies, one for each player, such that no player has an incentive (in terms of improving his own payoff) to deviate from his part of the strategy array.

32. Elsewhere, Hansen and I (1996, 56) have argued that this explanation can at least be consistent with government ownership's being efficiency-creating to the extent that it ties owners to those purchasing a product being produced by a firm. In this case, government ownership would also make predation less likely.

The government is probably also more diversified in its holdings and interests than many other organizations, though it seems unlikely to weight these holdings in the same way that the market does, and whatever advantage it has had in this respect has been declining over time.

Chapter Six

1. The social costs of public provision of higher education go well beyond the scope of this book, but they surely include the costs of government influencing the type of information that is produced (Lott 1990).

2. See Lott and Roberts 1991 for an example of how economists have failed to examine alternative competitive explanations for claims of price discrimination.

Appendix A

1. Staiger and Wolak (1989) construct a model in which anti-dumping cases may be filed (or threatened) by domestic firms not to respond to actual predatory behavior by foreign competitors, but rather to enforce an international cartel in which they are members. Their explanation appears to be inconsistent with the fact that, as section III(C) noted the majority of products subject to anti-dumping investigation are raw or relatively unprocessed commodities. Such products are expected to be the least susceptible to successful international cartelization.

2. Similarities in per capita GDP, production technologies, and product quality levels are among the criteria used to select an appropriate surrogate economy (Ehrenhaft 1989, 303–304).

3. See Vermulst 1989 and General Agreement on Tariffs and Trade 1970.

4. A different type of bias against nonmarket exporters could potentially arise if an exporting firm's pricing decision contained a random component. Instances of over-selling (price exceeding average cost) are ignored by the Department of Commerce in its adjudication of a dumping case. The department considers only instances of underselling in its calculations. This procedure implies that a firm whose export supply price varies over some range could be found guilty of dumping, even if its average price exceeded its constructed costs. This consideration does not present a problem for the current analysis. If I assume that consumers have complete information about the prices at which transactions occur, only random pricing decisions involving "too low" an offered price will result in consummated sales. Thus, the only occurrences of random pricing that I will observe in anti-dumping complaints will be those involving below-marginal cost sales. These cases will be included in the data set.

REFERENCES

Alchian, Armen A., and William R. Allen. 1983. *Exchange and Production: Competition, Coordination, and Control,* 3d edition. Belmont, Calif.: Wadsworth.

Alchian, Armen A., and Reuben A. Kessel. 1962. "Competition, Monopoly, and the Pursuit of Money." In *Aspects of Labor Economics, Special Conference Series.* Princeton: Princeton University Press for the National Bureau of Economic Research, 157–175.

Alexander, Cindy R., and Mark A. Cohen. 1996. "New Evidence on the Origins of Corporate Crime." *Managerial and Decision Economics* 17 (July–August 1996): 421–435.

Areeda, Phillip, and Donald F. Turner. 1975. "Predatory Pricing and Related Practices under Section 2 of the Sherman Act." *Harvard Law Review* 88 (February): 697–733.

Austin, Page. 1990. "Predatory Pricing Law since Matsushita." *Antitrust Law Journal* 58: 895–920.

Baker, Jonathan B. 1994. "Predatory Pricing after Brooke Group: An Economic Perspective." *Antitrust Law Journal* 62 (Spring): 26–44.

Baldwin, Robert E. 1988. *Trade Policy in a Changing World Economy.* Chicago: University of Chicago Press.

Barber, David H. 1987. *Securities Regulation.* Chicago: Harcourt Brace Jovanovich Legal and Professional Publications, 1987.

Bennett, James T., and Manuel H. Johnson. 1980. *The Political Economy of Federal Government Growth: 1959–1978.* College Station: Texas A&M University Press.

Bernheim, B. D. 1984. "Strategic Deterrence of Sequential Entry into an Industry." *Rand Journal of Economics* 15 (Spring): 40–65.

Binder, John J. 1988. "The Sherman Antitrust Act and the Railroad Cartels." *Journal of Law and Economics* 31, no. 2 (October): 443–468.

Bolton, Patrick, and David S. Scharfstein. 1990. "A Theory of Predation Based on Agency Problems in Financial Contracting." *American Economic Review* 80 (March): 93–106.

Borcherding, Thomas E. 1971. "A Neglected Social Cost of a Volunteer Military." *American Economic Review* 61, no. 1 (March): 195–196.

———, ed. 1977. *Budgets and Bureaucrats: The Sources of Government Growth.* Durham: Duke University Press.

———, Werner W. Pommerehne, and Bruner Schneider. 1982. "Comparing the

Efficiency of Private and Public Production: The Evidence from Five Countries." *Zeitschrift fur Nationalokonomie* 82: 235–275.

Bork, Robert H. 1978. *The Antitrust Paradox: A Policy at War with Itself.* New York: Basic Books.

Boschen, John F., and Kimberly J. Smith. 1995. "You Can Pay Me Now and You Can Pay Me Later: The Dynamic Response of Executive Compensation to Firm Performance." *Journal of Business* 68 (October): 577–608.

Boudreaux, Donald J., Kenneth G. Elzinga, and David E. Mills. 1995. "The Supreme Court's Predation Odyssey: From Fruit Pies to Cigarettes." *Supreme Court Economic Review* 4: 57–93.

Bresnahan, Timothy F. 1987. "Competition and Collusion in the American Automobile Industry: The 1955 Price War." *Journal of Industrial Economics* 35, no. 4 (June): 457–482.

Burnett, William B. 1994. "Predation by a Nondominant Firm: The Liggett Case (1993)." In *The Antitrust Revolution.*, ed. John E. Kwoka, Jr., and Lawrence J. White. New York: Scott Foresman, 2d ed.

Burns, Malcolm R. 1986. "Predatory Pricing and the Acquisition Cost of Competitors." *Journal of Political Economy* 94, no. 2 (April): 266–296.

———. 1989. "New Evidence on Predatory Price Cutting." *Managerial and Decision Economics* 10 (December): 327–330.

Carlton, Dennis W., and Daniel R. Fischel. 1983. "The Regulation of Insider Trading." *Stanford Law Review* 35 (May): 857–895.

Carlton, Dennis W., and Jeffrey M. Perloff. 1990. *Modern Industrial Organization.* Glenview, Ill.: Scott Foresman.

Central Intelligence Agency. 1980–1985. *World Factbook.* Washington, D.C.: Central Intelligence Agency.

Clark, William. 1988. "Production Costs and Output Qualities in Public and Private Employment Agencies." *Journal of Law and Economics* 31, no. 2 (October): 379–393.

Covault, Craig. 1989. "China Agrees to Limit Marketing of Long March Booster in U.S." *Aviation Week and Space Technology* 130 (January 21): 37.

Darby, Michael R., and John R. Lott, Jr. 1989. "Qualitative Information, Reputation, and Monopolistic Competition." *International Review of Law and Economics* 9, no. 1: 87–103.

David, Paul A. 1985. "Clio and the Economics of QWERTY." *American Economic Review* 75 (May): 332–337.

———. 1992. "Heroes, Herds, and Hysteresis in Technology History: Thomas Edison and 'The Battle of the Systems' Reconsidered." *Industrial & Corporate Change* 1: 120–137.

Davies, Stephen W., and Anthony J. McGuiness. 1982. "Dumping at Less than Marginal Cost." *Journal of International Economics* 12, nos. 1/2 (February): 169–182.

De Alessi, Louis. 1980. "The Economics of Property Rights: A Review of the Evidence." *Research in Law Economics* 2: 1–46.

———. 1982. "On the Nature and Consequences of Private and Public Enterprises." *Minnesota Law Review* 67 (October): 191–209.

DeAngelo, Harry, and Edward M. Rice. 1983. "Antitakeover Charter Amendments and Stockholder Wealth." *Journal of Financial Economics* 11: 329–360.

Demsetz, Harold. 1982a. "Barriers to Entry." *American Economic Review* 72, no. 1 (March): 47–57.

———. 1982b. *Economic, Legal, and Political Dimensions of Competition.* New York: North-Holland.

———, and Kenneth Lehn 1985. "The Structure of Corporate Ownership: Causes and Consequences." *Journal of Political Economy* 26 (December): 1155–1177.

Dunne, Nancy. 1990. "US Warns EC on Airbus Subsidies." *Financial Times,* September 8/9, p. 22.

Easterbrook, Frank H. 1981. "Predatory Strategies and Counterstrategies." *University of Chicago Law Review* 48 (Spring): 263–337.

———. 1984. "The Limits of Antitrust." *Texas Law Review* 63 (August): 1–40.

———. 1986. "On Identifying Exclusionary Conduct." *Notre Dame Law Review* 61: 972–980.

Ehrenhaft, Peter D. 1989. "The Application of Antidumping Duties to Imports from 'Nonmarket Economies.'" In *Antidumping Law and Practice: A Comparative Study,* ed. John H. Jackson and Edwin A. Vermulst. Ann Arbor: University of Michigan Press, 302–310.

Ellig, Jerome. 1989a. "Government and the Weather: The Privatization Option." Federal Privatization Project Issue Paper #109, Santa Monica, Calif.: Reason Foundation (August).

———. 1989b. "For Better Weather, Privatize." *Wall Street Journal,* December 4, p. A16.

Elzinga, Kenneth G. 1970. "Predatory Pricing: The Case of the Gunpowder Trust." *Journal of Law and Economics* 13, no. 1 (April): 223–240.

Finger, J. Michael, H. Keith Hall, and Douglas R. Nelson. 1982. "The Political Economy of Administered Protection." *American Economic Review* 72, no. 3 (June): 452–466.

Finger, J. Michael, and Andrezj Olechowski, eds. 1987. *The Uruguay Round: A Handbook on the Multilateral Trade Negotiations.* Washington, D.C.: The World Bank.

Foley, Theresa M. 1988. "U.S. Reviews Policy on Use of Chinese Launcher Following Export Requests." *Aviation Week and Space Technology,* August 1, 1988, 29.

Gastil, Raymond D. 1986. "The Comparative Survey of Freedom." *Freedom at Issue,* no. 88 (January/February): 3–16.

Gates, Susan, Paul Milgrom, and John Roberts. 1995. "Deterring Predation in Telecommunications: Are Line-of-Business Restrictions Needed?" *Managerial and Decision Economics* 16 (July–August): 427–438.

General Agreement on Tariffs and Trade. 1970. *Anti-Dumping Legislation.* Geneva: General Agreement on Tariffs and Trade.

Gifford, Daniel J. 1986. "The Role of the Ninth Circuit in the Development of the Law of Attempt to Monopolize." *Notre Dame Law Review* 61: 1021–1051.

Glazer, Kenneth L. 1994. "Predatory Pricing after Brooke Group: Predatory

Pricing and Beyond: Life after Brooke Group." *Antitrust Law Journal* 62 (Spring): 45–73.

Glosten, Lawrence R. 1989. "Insider Trading, Liquidity, and the Role of the Monopoly Specialist." *Journal of Business* 62: 78–97.

———, and L. Harris. 1988. "Estimating the Components of the Bid/Ask Spread." *Journal of Financial Economics* 21 (May): 135–156.

Granitz, Elizabeth, and Benjamin Klein. 1996. "Monopolization by 'Raising Rivals' Costs': The Standard Oil Case." *Journal of Law and Economics* 39: 1–48.

Grodinsky, Julius. 1957. *Jay Gould: His Business Career, 1867–1892.* Philadelphia: University of Pennsylvania Press.

Hansen, Robert G., and John R. Lott, Jr. 1995. "Profiting from Induced Changes in Competitors' Market Values: The Case of Entry and Entry Deterrence." *Journal of Industrial Economics* (September): 261–276.

Hansen, Robert G., and John R. Lott, Jr. 1996. "Externalities and Corporate Objectives in a World with Diversified Shareholder/Consumers." *Journal of Financial and Quantitative Analysis* 31, no. 1 (March): 43–68.

Hauser, Rolland K. 1985. *The Interface between Federal and Commercial Weather Services for Agricultural Industries—A Question of Policy.* Report prepared for the United States Department of Commerce, National Oceanic and Atmospheric Administration, Office of the Administrator. Washington, D.C. (November).

Hazlett, Thomas W. 1984. "Three Essays on Monopoly." Dissertation, University of California at Los Angeles.

———. 1985. "Private Contracting versus Public Regulation as a Solution to the Natural Monopoly Problem." In *Unnatural Monopolies: The Case for Deregulating Public Utilities,* ed. Robert W. Poole, Jr. Lexington, Mass.: Lexington Books, 71–114.

Hill, Steve. 1990a. "Merchants say A&M can hurt local business." *Bryan-College Station Eagle* (Texas) (May 20): A1, A4.

———. 1990b. "Businesses learn to live with A&M competition." *Bryan-College Station Eagle* (Texas) (May 22): A1, A3.

Hilton, George W. 1990. *American Narrow Gauge Railroads.* Stanford.: Stanford University Press.

Hirshleifer, Jack. 1971. "The Private and Social Value of Information and the Reward to Inventive Activity." *American Economic Review* 61: 561–574.

Holzman, Franklyn D. 1966. "Foreign Trade Behavior of Centrally Planned Economies." In *Industrialization in Two Systems,* ed. Henry Rosovsky, New York: John Wiley, 237–265.

Horlick, Gary. 1989. "The United States Antidumping System." In *Antidumping Law and Practice: A Comparative Study,* ed. John H. Jackson and Edwin A. Vermulst. Ann Arbor : University of Michigan Press, 56–72.

International Monetary Fund. 1987a, 1989. *Direction of Trade Yearbook,* Washington, D.C. : International Monetary Fund.

International Monetary Fund. 1987b. Supplement *on Public Sector Institutions,* Washington, D.C.: International Monetary Fund.

Isaac, R. Mark, and Vernon L. Smith. 1985. "In Search of Predatory Pricing." *Journal of Political Economy* 93, no. 2 (April): 320–345.

Jackson, John H. 1989a. "Dumping in International Trade: Its Meaning and Context." In *Antidumping Law and Practice: A Comparative Study,* ed, John H. Jackson and Edwin A. Vermulst. Ann Arbor: University of Michigan Press, 1–22.

———. 1989b. *The World Trading System: Law and Policy of International Economic Relations.* Cambridge: MIT Press.

Jensen, Michael C., and William H. Meckling. 1976. "Theory of the Firm: Managerial Behavior, Agency Costs, and Ownership Structure." *Journal of Financial Economics* 3: 305–360.

Jensen, Michael C., and Kevin Murphy. 1990. "Performance Pay and Top-Management Incentives." *Journal of Political Economy* 98 (April): 225–263.

Johnson, Ronald N. 1985. "U.S. Forest Service Policy and Its Budget." In *Forest Lands: Public and Private,* ed. Robert T. Deacon and M. Bruce Johnson. Boston: Ballinger.

———, and Gary D. Libecap. 1989a. "Bureaucratic Rules, Supervisor Behavior, and the Effect on Salaries in the Federal Government." *Journal of Law, Economics, and Organization* 5, no. 1 (Spring): 53–82.

———, and Gary D. Libecap. 1989b. "Agency Growth, Salaries and the Protected Bureaucrat." *Economic Inquiry* 27, no. 3 (July): 431–451.

Josephson, Matthew. 1934. *The Robber Barons.* New York: Harcourt, Brace.

Karpoff, Jonathan M., and John R. Lott, Jr. 1993. "The Reputational Penalty Firms Bear from Committing Criminal Fraud." *Journal of Law and Economics* 34 (October): 757–802.

Karpoff, Jonathan M., and Paul H. Malatesta. 1989. "The Wealth Effects of Second-Generation State Takeover Legislation." *Journal of Financial Economics* 25: 291–322.

Kenney, Roy W., and Benjamin Klein. 1983. "The Economics of Block Booking." *Journal of Law and Economics* 26, no. 2 (October): 479–540.

Kenny, Larry, and John R. Lott, Jr. 1996. "The Growth of Government and Giving Women the Right to Vote." University of Chicago Working Paper.

Khanna, Naveen, and Annette Poulsen. 1995. "Managers of Financially Distressed Firms: Villains or Scapegoats." *Journal of Finance* 50 (June): 919–940.

Klein, Benjamin. 1984. "Contract Costs and Administered Prices: An Economic Theory of Rigid Wages." *American Economic Review* 74 (May): 332–338.

———. 1996. "Why Hold-ups Occur: The Self-Enforcing Range of Contractual Relationships." *Economic Inquiry* 34, no. 3 (July): 444–463.

———, Robert G. Crawford, and Armen A. Alchian. 1978. "Vertical Integration, Appropriable Rents, and the Competitive Contracting Process." *Journal of Law and Economics* 21 (October): 297–326.

———, and Keith Leffler. 1981. "The Role of Market Forces in Assuring Contractual Performance." *Journal of Political Economy* 81 (August): 615–641.

Klein, Maury. 1986. *The Life and Legend of Jay Gould.* Baltimore: Johns Hopkins University Press.

Klein, William A., and J. Mark Ramseyer. 1994. *Business Associations: Agency, Partnerships, and Corporations.* Westbury, N.Y.: Foundation Press.

Klepper, Steve, and Edward E. Leamer. 1982. "Consistent Sets of Estimators for Regressions with Error in All Variables." *Econometrica* 50: 162–183.

Klevorick, Alvin K. 1993. "The Current State of the Law and Economics of Predatory Pricing." *American Economic Review* 83 (May): 162–167.

Knoeber, Charles R. 1986. "Golden Parachutes, Shark Repellents, and Hostile Tender Offers." *American Economic Review* 76 (March): 155–167.

Kolko, Gabriel. 1965. *Railroads and Regulation, 1877–1916.* New York: W. W. Norton.

Koller, Roland L. 1971. "The Myth of Predatory Pricing." *Antitrust Law and Economics Review* 4, no. 4 (Summer): 105–123.

Koopmans, T. C. 1937. *Linear Regression Analysis of Economic Time Series.* Amsterdam: Econometric Institute Haarlem–de Erwin F. Bohn N.V.

Kreps, David, and Robert Wilson. 1982. "Reputation and Imperfect Information." *Journal of Economic Theory* 27 (August): 253–279.

Langevourt, Donald C. 1986. *Insider Trading Handbook.* New York: Clark Boardman.

Lavergne, Réal P. 1983. *The Political Economy of U.S. Tariffs: An Empirical Analysis.* Toronto: Academic Press.

Leamer, Edward E. 1978. *Specification Searches: Ad Hoc Inferences with Non-experimental Data.* New York: John Wiley.

———. 1983. "Let's Take the Con Out of Econometrics." *American Economic Review* 27 (March): 31–43.

———. 1992. "Bayesian Elicitation Diagnostics." *Econometrica* 60, no. 4 (July): 919–942.

Libecap, Gary D. 1981. *Locking Up the Range.* Cambridge, Mass.: Ballinger.

Liebowitz, Stan, and Stephen E. Margolis. 1990. "Fable of the Keys." *Journal of Law and Economics* 33 (April): 1–25.

Liebowitz, Stan, and Stephen E. Margolis. 1995a. "Path Dependence, Lock-in, and History." *Journal of Law, Economics, and Organization* 11 (Spring): 205–226.

Liebowitz, Stan, and Stephen E. Margolis. 1995b. "Don't Handcuff Technology." *Upside Magazine,* September, 64–73.

Liebowitz, Stan, and Stephen E. Margolis. 1999. *From Qwerty to Microsoft: How Good Products Win in High Tech Markets.* San Francisco: Independent Institute.

Liebeler, Wesley. 1986. "Whither Predatory Pricing?: From Areeda and Turner to Matsushita." *Notre Dame Law Review* 61: 1052–1098.

Lindsay, M. Cotton. 1976. "A Theory of Government Enterprise." *Journal of Political Economy* 84, no. 5 (October): 1061–1077.

Linn, Scott C., and John J. McConnell. 1983. "An Empirical Investigation of the Impact of 'Antitakeover' Amendments on Common Stock Prices." *Journal of Financial Economics* 11: 361–400.

Logsdon, John M., and Ray A. Williamson. 1989. "U.S. Access to Space." *Scientific American* (March): 34–40.

Lopatka, John E., and William H. Page. 1995. "Microsoft, Monopolization, and

Network Externalities: Some Uses and Abuses of Economic Theory in Anti-trust Decision Making." *Antitrust Bulletin* 40, no. 2 (June 22): 2–34.

Lott, John R., Jr. 1987a. "Political Cheating." *Public Choice* 52, no. 2: 169–186.

———. 1987b. "Externalities, Agency Structure, and the Level of Transfers." *Public Choice* 53, no. 3: 285–287.

———. 1987c. "Why Is Education Publicly Provided?: A Critical Survey." *Cato Journal* 7, no. 2 (Fall): 475–501.

———. 1988. "Brand Names, Ignorance, and Quality Guaranteeing Premiums." *Applied Economics* 20, no. 2: 165–176.

———. 1990. "An Explanation for the Public Provision of Schooling: The Importance of Indoctrination." *Journal of Law and Economics* 33, no. 1 (April): 199–231.

———. 1996. "The Optimal Level of Criminal Fines in the Presence of Reputation." *Managerial and Decision Economics* 17 (July-August): 363–380.

———, and Stephen G. Bronars. 1993. "Time Series Evidence on Shirking in the U.S. House of Representatives." *Public Choice* 76, no. 1–2 (June): 125–150.

———, and Gertrud M. Fremling. 1989. "Time Dependent Information Costs, Price Controls, and Successive Government Intervention." *Journal of Law, Economics, and Organization* 5 (Fall): 293–306.

———, and W. Robert Reed. 1989. "Shirking and Sorting in a Model of Finite-Lived Politicians." *Public Choice* 61 (April): 75–96.

———, and Russell Roberts. 1991. "A Guide to the Pitfalls of Identifying Price Discrimination." *Economic Inquiry* 29, no. 1 (January): 14–23.

Maddala, G. S. 1983. *Limited Dependent and Qualitative Variables in Econometrics.* Cambridge: Cambridge University Press.

Magee, Stephen P., and Leslie Young. 1987. "Endogenous Protection in the United States, 1900–1984." In *U.S. Trade Policies in a Changing World Economy*, ed. Robert M. Stern. Cambridge: MIT Press, 145–195.

Malatesta, Paul H., and Ralph A. Walking. 1988. "Poison Pill Securities: Stockholder Wealth, Profitability, and Ownership Structure." *Journal of Financial Economics* 20: 347–376.

Manne, Henry G. 1966. *Insider Trading and the Stock Market.* New York: Free Press.

Mastanduno, Michael 1988. "The Management of Alliance Export Control Policy: American Leadership and the Politics of COCOM." In *Controlling East-West Trade and Technology Transfer*, ed. Gary K. Bertsch. Durham: Duke University Press, 241–279.

McGee, John S. 1958. "Predatory Price Cutting: The Standard Oil (N.J.) Case." *Journal of Law and Economics* 1, no. 1 (October): 137–169.

———. 1980. "Predatory Pricing Revisited." *Journal of Law and Economics* 23, no. 2 (October): 289–330.

Mecham, Michael. 1987. "U.S., Europe Seek Rapid Cure in Airbus Subsidy Dispute," *Aviation Week & Space Technology* (October 26): 35, 39.

Meulbroek, Lisa K., Mark L. Mitchell, J. Harold Mulherin, Jeffrey M. Netter, and Annette B. Poulsen. 1990. "Shark Repellents and Managerial Myopia: An Empirical Test." *Journal of Political Economy* 98 (October): 1108–1117.

Milgrom, Paul, and John Roberts. 1982a. "Limit Pricing and Entry under Incomplete Information: An Equilibrium Analysis." *Econometrica* 50 (October): 443–460.

Milgrom, Paul, and John Roberts. 1982b. "Predation, Reputation and Entry Deterrence." *Journal of Economic Theory* 27 (August): 280–312.

Morck, R., Andrei Shleifer, and Robert Vishny. 1989. "Alternative Mechanisms of Corporate Control." *American Economic Review* 79 (September): 842–852.

Muraoka, Dennis D., and Richard B. Watson. 1985. "Economic Issues in Federal Timber Sale Procedure." In *Forest Lands: Public and Private,* ed. Robert T. Deacon and M. Bruce Johnson. Boston: Ballinger.

Murphy, Kevin J. 1985. "Corporate Performance and Managerial Remuneration: An Empirical Analysis." *Journal of Accounting and Economics* 7: 12–41.

National Park Service. 1989. Single Visit Rates FY 1986, FY 1987, and FY 1989, National Park Service / United States Department of Interior, Statistical Office, Denver Service Center.

Niskanen, William A. 1971. *Bureaucracy and Representative Government.* Chicago: Aldine Atherton .

———. 1974. "Comment." *Public Choice* 17, no. 1: 43–45.

———. 1975. "Bureaucrats and Politicians." *Journal of Law and Economics* 18, no. 3 (December): 617–643.

North, Douglass C. 1991. *Institutions, Institutional Change, and Economic Performance.* New York: Cambridge University Press.

Olson, Mancur, Jr., and Richard Zeckhauser. 1966. "An Economic Theory of Alliances." *The Review of Economics and Statistics* 48, no. 3 (August): 266–279.

Ordover, Janusz A., and Garth Saloner. 1989. "Predation, Monopolization, and Antitrust." In *Handbook of Industrial Organization,* ed. Richard Schmalensee and Robert Willig. New York: Elsevier Science.

Palmeter, N. David. 1989. "The Impact of the U.S. Anti-dumping Law on China-U.S. Trade." *Journal of World Trade* 23: 5–14.

Parsons, Donald O., and Edward John Ray. 1975. "The United States Steel Consolidation: The Creation of Market Control." *Journal of Law and Economics* 18, no. 1 (April): 181–220.

Peltzman, Sam. 1991. "The Handbook of Industrial Organization: A Review Article." *Journal of Political Economy* 99, no. 1 (February): 201–217.

Priest, George, and Benjamin Klein. 1984. "The Selection of Disputes for Litigation." *Journal of Legal Studies* 13 (June): 1–45.

Porter, Robert H. 1983. "A Study of Cartel Stability: The Joint Executive Committee, 1880–1886." *The Bell Journal of Economics* 14, no. 2 (Autumn): 301–314.

Posner, Richard A. 1976. *Antitrust Law.* Chicago: University of Chicago Press.

Prusa, Thomas J. 1989. "Why Are So Many Antidumping Petitions Withdrawn?" State University of New York at Stony Brook Working Paper, no. 326.

Rasmusen, Eric. 1988. "Entry for Buyout." *Journal of Industrial Economics* 36 (March) : 281–300.

———. 1989. *Games and Information: An Introduction to Game Theory.* New York: Basil Blackwell.

———. 1991. "Signal Jamming and Limit Pricing: A Unified Approach." Yale Law School Working Paper.

Ray, Edward John. 1981. "The Determinants of Tariff and Nontariff Trade Restrictions in the United States." *Journal of Political Economy* 89, no. 1 (February): 105–121.

Reback, Gary L., Susan Creighton, David Killam, Neil Nathanson, Garth Saloner and W. Brian Arthur. 1995. "Why Microsoft Must Be Stopped." *Upside Magazine,* February, 52–67.

Roberts, John. 1986. "A Signaling Model of Predatory Pricing." *Oxford Economic Papers* (Supplement) 38: 75–93.

Ruffenach, Glenn. 1989. "Air Express Firms Sue Postal Service on Overseas Rates." *Wall Street Journal,* October 13, A4.

Salop, Steven C., and David T. Scheffman. 1987. "Cost-Raising Strategies." *Journal of Industrial Economics* 36 (January): 19–34.

Salvatore, Dominick. 1989. "A Model of Dumping and Protectionism in the United States." *Weltwirtschaftliches Archives* 125, no. 4: 763–781.

Salwen, Kevin. 1991. "SEC to Air Short Sales Registration." *Wall Street Journal,* June 7, C1.

Shapiro, Carl. 1983. "Premiums for High Quality Products as Rents to Reputation." *Quarterly Journal of Economics* 98: 659–680.

———. 1989. "Theories of Oligopolistic Behavior." In *The Handbook of Industrial Organization,* ed. Richard Schmalensee and Robert D. Willig. Amsterdam: North-Holland, 1989.

Shaw, Jane, and Richard L. Stroup. 1989. "Who Pays the Piper Calls the Tune." PERC Viewpoints. Bozeman, Mont.: Political Economy Research Center, April 5.

Staiger, Robert W., and Frank A. Wolak. 1989. "Strategic Use of Antidumping Law to Enforce Tacit International Collusion." National Bureau of Economic Research Working Paper, no. 3016.

Stigler, George J. 1965. "The Dominant Firm and the Inverted Umbrella." *Journal of Law and Economics* 8 (October): 167–172.

Stiglitz, Joseph E. 1992. "Another Century of Economic Science." In *The Future of Economics,* ed. John D. Hey. Cambridge, Mass., and Oxford: Blackwell.

Stillman, Robert S. 1983. "Examining Antitrust Policy Towards Horizontal Mergers." *Journal of Financial Economics* 11: 225–240.

Summers, Robert, and Alan Heston. 1988. "A New Set of International Comparisons of Real Products and Prices: Estimates for 130 Countries, 1950–1985." *Review of Income and Wealth* 34, no. 1 (March): 1–26.

Takacs, Wendy E. 1981. "Pressures for Protectionism: An Empirical Analysis." *Economic Inquiry* 19, no. 4 (October): 687–693.

Telser, Lester. 1966. "Cutthroat Competition and the Long Purse." *Journal of Law and Economics* 9 (October): 259–277.

Tirole, Jean. 1990. *The Theory of Industrial Organization.* Cambridge: MIT Press.

Treynor, Jack, and Fisher Black. 1973. "How to Use Security Analysis to Improve Portfolio Selection." *Journal of Business* 46, no. 1 (January): 1–32.

United Nations. 1986. *National Accounts Statistics: Main Aggregates and Detailed Tables.* New York: United Nations.

United Nations. 1988. *1986 International Trade Statistics Yearbook.* New York: United Nations.

United Nations Conference on Trade and Development. 1981, 1984, 1985. *Handbook of International Trade and Development Statistics.* New York: United Nations.

United Nations Conference on Trade and Development. 1984–1989. *Problems of Protectionism and Structural Adjustment.* Geneva: United Nations.

United States, Department of Commerce. 1989. *Statistical Abstract of the United States: 1989.* Washington, D.C.: G.P.O.

United States, International Trade Commission. 1985. *Operation of the Trade Agreements Program.* Washington, D.C.: G.P.O.

United States, International Trade Commission. 1987. *Annual Report.* Washington, D.C.: G.P.O.

United States Postal Service. 1973. Statutes Restricting Private Carriage of Mail and Their Administration, House Committee on Post Office and Civil Service, 93rd Cong., 1st Session, Committee Print, 6.

Vermulst, Edwin A. 1989. "The Antidumping Systems of Australia, Canada, the EEC, and the USA: Have Antidumping Laws Become a Problem in International Trade?" In *Antidumping Law and Practice: A Comparative Study,* ed. John H. Jackson and Edwin A. Vermulst. Ann Arbor: University of Michigan Press, 425–466.

Vita, Michael G., and Charissa P. Wellford. 1994. "Regulating the Electromagnetic Environment: Alternative Approaches to Policy." In *Science, Technology, and the Environment,* ed. James R. Fleming & Henry A. Gemery. Akron, Oh.: University of Akron Press.

Wang, William K. S. 1996. "Insider Trading." Unpublished manuscript, Boston.

Weiman, David, and Richard Levin. 1994. "Preying for Monopoly?: The Case of the Southern Bell Telephone Company, 1894–1912." *Journal of Political Economy* 102 (February): 103–126.

Wilczynski, Jozef. 1966a. "Dumping and Central Planning." *Journal of Political Economy* 74, no. 3 (June): 250–264.

———. 1966b. "Dumping in Trade between Market and Centrally Planned Economies." *Economics of Planning* 6, no. 3: 211–227.

———. 1969. *The Economics and Politics of East-West Trade.* New York: Praeger.

Wiley, John Shepard, Jr. 1986. "A Capture Theory of Antitrust Federalism." *Harvard Law Review* 99, no. 4 (February): 713–789.

Wilson, James Q. 1989. *Bureaucracy.* New York: Basic Books.

Wittman, Donald. 1985. "Is the Selection of Cases for Trial Biased?" *Journal of Legal Studies* 14 (January): 185–221.

Wolf, Thomas A. 1988. *Foreign Trade in the Centrally Planned Economy.* Bern, Switzerland: Harwood Academic.

Yamey, Basil S. 1972. "Predatory Price Cutting: Notes and Comments." *Journal of Law and Economics* 15, no. 1 (April): 129–142.

A. A. Poultry Farms, Inc. v. Rose Acre Farms, Inc. (1989), 7
Agencies, government
  absence of evaluation of, 67
  advantages in predatory actions, 149n4
  benefits from deterring entry, 144n7
  driving new entrant from market, 65
  with elimination of private competitors, 67–68
  maximizing output, 3–4, 61, 63–65
  predation by small, 71–72
  price discrimination by, 68–70
  pricing output below market and below cost, 64–68, 74
  profit maximization by, 65
  returns to predation, 61, 67
  social cost of predation for small and large, 66, 71–73
  See also Cross-subsidization
Alchian, Armen A., 5
Alexander, Cindy R., 60
Allen, William R., 5
American Airlines, 133n11
American Tobacco Company predatory pricing, 116
Anti-dumping complaints
  countries in sample of, 126
  against firms in market and non-market economies, 79–87

Note: t denotes "table."

political influence affecting, 87–91
  as threats, 145n13
  treatment of subsidies in, 123
  See also Dumping complaints
Anti-dumping laws
  enforcement of, 78
  intent of, 123
  remedies under, 75
Antitakeover laws, state-level
  firms in states with, 50–52
  potential predators reincorporating under, 24
  predatory firms in states without, 60
Antitrust laws
  cases decided under (1890–1965), 9–10
  exemption of government-owned enterprises from, 74, 77–78
  intent of enforcement, 122
  merger guidelines, 71
  standards in Alcoa case (1945), 135n22
Austin, Page, 28, 29–30t

Baker, Jonathan B., 6, 133n10
Barber, David H., 107
Best, Alan, 105
Binder, John J., 116
Bolton, Patrick, 26
Bork, Robert H., 1, 10, 60, 71
Bresnahan, Timothy, 132n7
Brooke Group Ltd. v. Brown & Williamson Tobacco Corp. (1993), 10–12, 134nn13, 14, 17, 18, 138n15

Managers
  barriers to removal, 24–25
  compensation in periods of al-
    leged predation, 36–46, 120
  compensation during predatory
    periods, 26–27, 120
  credible predatory commitments
    of, 59, 120
  in firms with R&D investments,
    24
  incentives for creating reputation
    for toughness, 19–27, 120
  prediction of leaving or removal,
    56–59, 120
  strategies of managers in public
    agencies, 3–4
  support for tough manager the-
    ory, 56
  testing predicted removal of,
    49–59
Margolis, Stephen E., 13, 14, 15, 16,
  136nn26, 28, 29
Market economies. *See* Economies,
  market
Market entry
  credibility of commitment to, 113
  cross-trading stock, 110–12
  effect of trading profits on proba-
    bility of, 98–99
  with entry-deterring incumbent,
    113–15
  of Kodak into instant photogra-
    phy market, 97–98
  models, 109–15
  new firm incentives for, 65
  with price discrimination, 70
  profits for entrant and incumbent,
    108
  short selling to achieve, 103–5
  with threat of dumping, 144n7
  trading profit effect on probability
    of, 115
Market entry deterrence
  effect of trading profits on proba-
    bility of, 99

  incumbent and predator firms in,
    98–99
  models, 109–15
  profitability of, 127–30
Material injury requirement, 124
*Matsushita Elec. Indus. Co. v. Zenith
  Radio Corp.* (1986), 1, 10, 134n16,
  138n15
Mecham, Michael, 75
Mergers
  antitrust guidelines, 71
  incentives for, 100
  prices firms pay in, 117
Microsoft
  alleged bundling, 12–13, 135n25
  alleged predatory behavior, 10–15
  alleged tying, 15–16
  monopoly power of, 15
Milgrom, Paul, 1–2, 3, 16, 18, 63
Misappropriation theory
  accepted by Supreme Court, 107
  related to stolen information, 106
Monopoly
  Microsoft's power, 15
  natural, 13
  Polaroid's position, 96–97
Muraoka, Dennis D., 69
Murphy, Kevin J., 39

Nash equilibrium, 153n31
Nelson, Douglas R., 82
Niskanen, William, 63, 64, 65, 67, 73,
  74, 142nn9, 13, 143n16
Nonmarket economies. *See* Econo-
  mies, nonmarket
North, Douglass, 135n24

Olechowski, Andrezj, 79, 80t, 94, 123
Opler, Tim, x
Ordover, Janusz A., 2, 26

Page, William H., 13
Park, Trenor W., 103–5
Parsons, Donald O., 116
Peltzman, Sam, x, 4–5